THE ENERGY OF *Creativity*

Editor
Erica Glessing

THE ENERGY OF CREATIVITY
Edited by Erica Glessing

The Energy of Creativity
Compiled by Erica Glessing
Copyright 2016 by Happy Publishing, Erica Glessing
First Edition
ISBN: 978-0-9961712-5-0

Original cover painting by Tara Thelen
http://tara-artwork.com

Cover design by Deborah Perdue
www.IlluminationGraphics.com
Interior Design by Roseanna White Designs

Edited by Betsy McLoughlin

No part of this publication may be translated, reproduced or transmitted in any form without prior permission in writing from the publisher.

Publisher and editor are not liable for typographical errors, content mistakes, inaccuracies, or omissions related to the information in this book.

All of the contributors to this publication have granted permission for inclusion.

Product trade names or trademarks mentioned throughout this publication remain property of their respective owners.

Published by Happy Publishing, www.HappyPublishing.net

Foreword

THE ENERGY OF CREATION IS LIFE-GIVING

Many people believe that creative energy is only useful for doing something 'in the arts', but did you know that it's actually what we use to create our lives every day? You use it when you are working at your job, you use it when you are caring for your children, and you use it when you are re-organizing your sock drawer!

Creative energy is life force energy. It is big, expansive and it makes things grow. When we put it consciously to use in our lives, we make the seemingly impossible happen with total ease. Creating is as natural to us as breathing. Creation is not work. It does not take what we traditionally think of as effort, and in fact, since our natural state is that of a creative being, the creation of anything can be easy, and really, really fun!

Have you ever watched a toddler with a crayon and a piece of paper? The first thing you see is the little face light up with joy. They look at every color, and they choose one, and squeal happily, and race the crayon across the page. They go on to another color, and another and another, and the lines get bigger and bolder and faster.

Does that look like work? Does it look 'serious'?

Creative energy is the energy of play. It is present in everything at all times. It is the constant invitation to truly enjoy your life in every moment and create it consciously as you go along.

This book offers you many such moments, written by people who are masters of creation—who live by it! They share life changing stories, and show you how you can be present in the creation of your life at all times.

Enjoy these chapters, and I hope you accept this beautiful invitation to put creative energy to use in your life—in every colorfully delicious way!

Cheri L. R. Taylor
Writing and Creativity Coach
Radio Host, *Creative Energy in YOU*
on the A2zen.fm Radio Network
CheriLRTaylor.com

Table of Contents

Chapter 1..7
FINDING YOUR CREATIVE PROCESS
Alex Ava Kimball

Chapter 2
INTANGIBLE INSANITY –
A DIFFERENT SOURCE POINT OF CREATIVITY.................23
Rebecca Hulse

Chapter 3
CREATIVITY EXPONENTIALIZED:
EXPLORING THE BIG PICTURE...39
Meredith Locher

Chapter 4
THE POWER OF WORDS TO CREATE...................................49
Megan Walrod

Chapter 5
THE MAGIC OF CREATIVITY..61
Katherine McIntosh

Chapter 6
UNLOCK YOUR CREATIVITY, UNLOCK YOUR
EMOTIONS..77
Laura Hackel

Chapter 7
CREATIVITY: THE INFINITE SPACE OF
INFINITE POSSIBILITY.......................................87
Dr. Lisa Cooney

Chapter 8
LUSCIOUS LEADERSHIP......................................97
Danna Lewis

Chapter 9
CREATIVITY IS MAGIC......................................105
Tara Thelen

Chapter 10
CO-CREATING WITH YOUR GUIDES AND ANGELS........109
Andy Pentecost

CHAPTER 11
CREATIVITY IS EVERYWHERE..........................123
Deborah Perdue

Chapter 12
THE ADVENTURES OF CREATIVITY................131
Betsy McLoughlin

Chapter 13
BORN TO BE CREATIVE....................................143
By Erica Glessing

Chapter 1

FINDING YOUR CREATIVE PROCESS

By Alex Ava Kimball

It's really funny, but I never thought I had a creative process until I heard others telling me that they couldn't possibly do what I do. I thought, you're crazy this is so easy! I used to also think you had to struggle and that things needed to be difficult. If something was easy I couldn't possibly be actually doing it, right? Before I continue I want to ask you something. I want to talk right now to you, that beautiful all-knowing being that is you. I want to connect with you on an authentic level. I long to interface with you, your spirit, your soul, your being, that deepest truth that is you.

Hello, welcome! It's so nice to connect with you with such a moving and desiring intensity. Throughout the following text, I have asked a lot of questions. In order to derive the maximum benefit to these questions, I suggest reading them a few times. After each question, stop reading further, take a deep breath, and look away, let your mind and body wander and ponder with the question. The point is not to find or arrive at the answer or solution immediately. I'm inviting you on a journey to bathe yourself in the question. At the same time, I'm asking you to ponder, and dwell, to escape to a fantasy of possibilities. Ask the questions with a curiosity of inquiring without trying to work out the answers. I want you to just let go and just be. This is not a brainstorming session. My driving desire for you is to surrender, and breathe deeply into the questions. Maintain this inquiring curiosity after you've read the question, and allow your gaze to behold you! You may feel sleepy while asking a question. That's great, if so, than sleep and take a nap. It may be what your body is requiring. The objective is not to look to conclude the space to a standstill or gridlock. My wish for you is that you take care of you, the being that is truly you in a cherished honouring of the magnificence of you. I long for you to find enrichment with special attention being giving to your desires. I yearn for you to whet your appetite and find that special place in you that you've forgotten and kept hidden. That's the element of you that is demanding to be treated with tenderness.

What I Know for Sure

What I know for sure is everybody is magnificent and great at something. Something you do so well with such ease that you have previously criticized and think has no value. Others can see it in you; they appreciate it and maybe even adore you because of it. Somewhere we've bought the lie that if you do something with such grace and ease it must not have value. Then we lumber through things that are difficult for us and we despise every moment of it. Wondering what are we doing wrong, other people seem to be managing. Well so it seems on the outside. None of us truly have the opportunity of seeing everything about what someone goes through in life and I'm pretty sure you don't really want to. We've all seen other people around us have difficult lives; maybe you've encountered hindrances as well. Some of us go to school, get a degree, get a great job whether we like it or not. Then one day wake up miserable, suffering depression and wondering what we did wrong. What if you did nothing wrong? What if life was about choosing? What if, at any point, you could just make a choice to do something else? If that didn't work out or you didn't like it, you just chose something else. What if none of your choices were wrong choices, just choices? What if you accepted those choices as another way of receiving information, and said "thank you"?

These days we barely give ourselves time to even think about what we truly desire to create in the world. Everyone has a unique quality about them even if you don't think so. This is what makes us unique. So first, what do you desire to create that would truly make your heart sing? What is that one thing or maybe there are many things that you feel deep inside you, that if you don't do something now you are going to die?

**What is it you would like to create?
I wonder what that would look like!**

I want you to remember back when you were a small child, you were so happy with what you were doing, you just had so much energy and you didn't want to stop. You didn't want to wait till you were grown up. It made no sense to you as a child. I didn't want to go to school; I was bored and had many debates with teachers about certain subjects at school. I learned not to tell people what I really wanted to do, not to waste your time that was just not sensible. Who do you think you are? Or perhaps you never had a happy childhood. Well, it's time to move on and create the life you want right now. Let's not live in the past and feel we have to maintain those rules of what I wasn't able to do, or what encouragement I never received. How much longer are you going to let this control the rest of your life? Would you like to stop living your life through someone else's eyes of what's expected of you? Furthermore it's a different world now, and so much is changing with an endless stream and avenues to explore? Many people are growing restless and changing their direction in life because it's not the life they wanted. They don't even know what they want but the way they are living is not working for them.

Have you ever contemplated or fantasized about the kind of a life that would be fun to live? Wouldn't you love to explore creating? On your terms? I wonder what that could possibly look like for you.

Playtime

Hmmm, remember play? When is the last time you played with the idea of just letting loose? It's in the exploring of our desires, whether it's writing, singing, skateboarding, playing an instrument, painting, teaching, or playing with kids.

So let's have a look at finding your creative process:

People think to be a creator of something you have to be talented. I'm going to tell you something you might never have heard before. Even though we've never met, I know you already are exceptional at something. I bet there are quite a few things you do extremely well that you have ignored. How do I know this? I've never met someone who isn't brilliant at something. There's a gift we all were born with, whether you believe me or not. Think about friends you have or people you briefly met. Have you ever thought wow! They are so talented, maybe they're funny or a charismatic story teller. Possibly you have seen a parent or a friend that no matter what life threw at them, they always managed to land on their feet. Not to mention someone who can paint or draw, or a singer, or a dancer. Someone who inspires or motivates very naturally. Those people who are athletically skilled or someone who has a sense of ease and joy with technology. Maybe someone who is constantly inventive, they can just come up with creative ideas with finesse and ease. They may have what the French call, 'je ne sais quoi', that undefinable something.

Are you still with me?

What if there was no separation between living and creating? What if creating is not just about you being the greatest artist or an award writing novelist? What if there is an endless supply of creative energy all around you constantly? We learn to shut down parts of our self and build walls because we believed these so called criticisms or judgments. Or we simply have been the one doing most of the judging. What if all of this is a downright lie?

What if you stopped defending what they said or what you've convinced yourself is true? What would you choose instead?

Let's pretend you are about five years old. I want you to take some time and write down things you did then? When there was no goal involved. You just woke up in the morning and couldn't finish breakfast fast enough, you didn't want to brush your teeth. You might of hated having to change out of your pajamas because that was going to cut into your curiosity of the day. You hated being called in for lunch or dinnertime, let alone take a bath despite being covered in dirt and grass in your hair. I used to think, are you kidding me, I'm having such a great time out here playing with my friends. Let alone come night time you now had to sleep. Good grief, what for? I don't need sleep you would declare! You felt like you might possibly miss something truly great. If you have children, maybe you've encountered this behavior with them.

Here's a small list of things that I used to do when I was a kid:

- Played dress ups
- Built cubby houses
- Rode my bike
- Fantasized I was an actress and made up scenes
- Kicked a ball around
- Played with my siblings or neighbors kids
- Played with the cat
- Played with my dog
- Laid in the grass, rolled around in it
- Laid on the grass at night and counted stars
- Made up stories in my head with what the clouds looked like

- Would spin around as fast as I could like a bottle top and fall down and watch everything around me moving

- Made mud pies

- Played tea parties

- Made crowns and jewelry out of clover

- Skipped rope.

- Played hopscotch

- Sang into my hairbrush in front of the mirror

- Played with dolls

- Played cricket with my brother

- Coloured in

It's your turn - write your list of things you did when you were young. Find somewhere comfortable and remember being that young child. How did you fill your day? Write it down even if it seems silly. It is required to escape and be as silly as possible.

Do you notice you did things for no other reason other than they were fun and made you happy until they didn't? You would just change and do something else. You had played with dolls and now you wanted to build a cubby or tree house. You knew when it was time to colour in or play with the next-door neighbour. You did all these things until you decided you wanted to do something else. You just wanted to explore different things; you kept looking for what was going to be fun. As children we are so curious about everything. Something happens along the way and we tend to stop having that inquisitive nature.

If you look at your list, you will notice the emphasis was clearly on play.

What if you could start adding some of those things again in your life? I wonder what would happen?

For me, when I'm feeling a little bored or just out of sorts, I know I need to change something. I've done these things often enough now that I know if I were to go to the botanical gardens for a walk, I will feel better. Or take myself to the movies. Read a book, do my yoga. Go for a swim, or just lie in the sun. Go roller blading; catch up with a friend for a chat. Or simply sit alone at a coffee shop and do some people watching. I'm not trying to occupy my mind, when I'm doing these things. I feel it is my body that wants a date with fun. I can sense tenseness and an uneasy out of sorts' kind of feeling. Feeling frustrated, upset, angry, and sometimes nothing is particularly wrong in my world. My body is requiring some time out and sustenance that is unquantifiable.

We become so uncomfortable with these feelings and sensations in our body that we've forgotten how to take care of it. We will try and push it aside through eating or a myriad of the addictive substance or activities that seem to take that feeling away for a moment. Another failed attempt at diverting what we have decided is wrongness about us. Instead of making yourself wrong because we don't understand this discomfort, what if I said by playing with these ideas you could get to connecting with the little child inside of you that does know what you enjoyed doing? You might attempt some of these activities and decide you don't like to do them anymore. That's fine, these are only ideas to move you forward to keep explor-

The Energy of Creativity

ing like you did when you were younger. The only goal is to unhook and unleash from the usual mundane of "doing," to get to the playfulness of "being" like you were when you were a kid.

I wonder what you knew about you way back then, that you've hidden somewhere deep inside you? Did you already know what you came here to do? Did you already know what made you happy and stopped doing it because life simply got in the way?

Next I'm going to show you an example of creating something out of seemingly nothing. Are you fascinated to see how that is possible? Let's venture into a deeper place of discovering more of you and your hidden talents. I double dog dare you to go further.

If you're still here I'll let you in on something already. You are already doing what I call 'following the energy'. It's nothing difficult or mysterious, it's actually a very natural way of living. When something interests you, you will stay with it. You don't know what it is but something is pulling you to follow it. You can't put that favourite book down. You can't let go of that strange feeling you have that you cannot describe with words. It's either exciting you, making you angry and upset or there's a welling up inside of you that wants to be expressed and you just don't know what to do.

When we repress or push down these things inside and bury them, they can literally make us sick. We may have spent a life time of ignoring or pushing aside a lot of information to such a point that we've assumed something was really wrong with us. We went to doctors and psychiatrists looking for answers, not that they cannot be helpful, but could it be that truly something has been going on inside of us that we have never addressed? Did we know something when we were little children, a skill of perception that was never encouraged or advised to explore? Maybe our loved ones or our teachers also cut off that part of themselves. Let's say for arguments sake they ignored these places in them and buried them to get on with their life. It's hard to turn to someone for guidance with these very people hiding their own possibly great potentials from themselves.

What if you already knew what you wanted to do and how you wanted to live your life?

Let's go back to what I was calling following the energy. It can be called many things like listening to the whisperings or hearing the call. Just for arguments sake, I'm calling it following the energy and please don't make it too significant. You all do this naturally.

Do you recall when someone told you about a strange occurrence that happened to them? You were so intrigued with their electrifying story that you were hanging on every word and almost holding your breath with excitement? Coupled with their delivery and excitement they were exuding, you couldn't help but be drawn into their vivid story telling. Or maybe you were watching a horror movie that you were so captivated by and almost holding your breath, than let out a scream or jumped. That's what I mean by following the energy. You've become so engrossed with what's happening, you could not turn away.

Have you ever been with a group of people and there was a conversation going on and inside you were dying to say something but didn't? Again, following the energy.

Maybe you disagreed wholeheartedly with everything that was being said, and you stayed silent. Maybe you also knew that if you interjected your thoughts they wouldn't be received. Possibly you had previously done so with your thoughts and you were accused of something, or made to feel wrong. Or everyone laughed at you and it made you feel insecure. It was at that point you decided that's it. I'm never going to share my opinion again. Burnt one too many times and thought it's not worth it. I think we've all been there in some way or form. I left the party and lamented over what I should of or could have said myself for a night, or a week, sometimes longer.

What if there was a way you could express yourself that would possibly help you nurture that unexpressed element of you? Let's have a look at finding ways to harness this energy constructively.

I want you to go back to the list you've already written above, and see if there is one thing that you wish to do again. For me, it's singing along to music into my hairbrush in front of the mirror, for no other reason than its fun for me. I don't have to tell anyone that I'm doing it. I'm just going to explore singing into my hairbrush. My make shift microphone lets me escape to a space of daydreaming and imaging. I totally let go, no one is watching, that I'm aware of. Many times during and after my playtime, I am bombarded with impulsive and extraordinary ideas of things to do or what I could create. Remember, you are only doing this for one reason and one reason only, and that's to play. Play, play, and play. Try adding play into your everyday life; you will discover you're living an adventurous life unlike many people around you.

I would recommend doing one of these activities every day if possible. You can slowly build up to an hour a day or every few days at least. It can be anything; it's about discovering what you might like to do. Not what you've already decided you like to do. You need to discover silly things that you wouldn't necessarily do for simply the joy or fun of it. Not because you have to do it, but because if you were 5 again, you would do it. I've discovered inspiration comes from everything I do that is fun for me. Whether it is sitting and reading in solitude with a great book or doing something physical like dancing.

I recommend you have somewhere you can log all these crazy ideas in a book or keep in your notes section of your phone. Don't panic if you don't get anything. It may take time for you to really let go and escape the monkey mind. It's best to put your entries into a place that's always handy. So the moment you get an idea, you write it down. That's why I suggest your smart phone or diary. Whatever works for you. Now these ideas could be from I need to go get a particular book from a bookstore or an idea to start a business.

I want you to list that entire screwball, zany and wacky ideas that seem so foreign to you but make you laugh and you may even think you couldn't possibly do. It's about being as out-there, insane, bonkers and just plain weird as possible.

What I have found is there becomes a theme of certain ideas that keep coming back to the forefront of your imagination.

So you might not discover the new anti-aging solution, and then again you just might. What if the actual seed was the creative thought they you received before you wrote it down? Once you write it down, it's like something a bit more concrete is in play that wasn't there before. Now you are doing a dance with the insight you received. I'm not saying that writing it down will make it happen. I am saying that writing it down allows you to amuse yourself with the inklings. Now you really would have to start to take notice of while you were playing, (colouring in, playing a sport, reading, being in nature or whatever's on your list) the similar desires or dreams start to repeat themselves. It's like there seems to be some kind of magical force in play that was kept hidden. It's only hidden because you've spent a lifetime of stuffing down the things inside you that you said you didn't have time for or didn't make sense to you. Is now the time these things wish to see the light? If you play with this space of discovery, I promise you this will open up a deep longing that has been trying to get out. Maybe, just maybe, your whole life will change beyond anything you never knew was possible.

Please keep in touch and let me know how the process is going for you. I would love to share more and inspire you to take steps further into this exciting unknown place of being.

About the Author

ALEX AVA KIMBALL

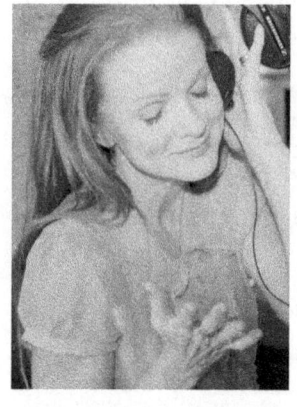

Alex Ava Kimball is creator of Artistic Verve, a safe and caring place for you to discover and communicate your uniqueness in the world.

Alex has been a life-long dreamer and explorer of the human journey. Raised in a beach side provincial town near Brisbane Australia, Alex has travelled and lived in Australia, Japan, the United States and currently residing with her husband in Singapore.

Alex has always worked professionally in the arts from musical theatre to her first love, singing jazz. This is where she has honed her love of the creative arts and mind, always seeking out the inner gifts in her and in those she meets. Drawn to creativity and moving others, she recently began writing her experiences and hopes her motivations will drive others to also look within and question, seek and never stop dreaming.

She is an Access Consciousness® facilitator.

Alex believes in order to live a fulfilling life we must always be creating.

Website: https://www.artisticverve.com

Email: alex_kimball@hotmail.com

Facebook: https://www.facebook.com/public/Alex-Kimball

Chapter 2

INTANGIBLE INSANITY – A DIFFERENT SOURCE POINT OF CREATIVITY

By Rebecca Hulse

"What is creativity? Creativity is the vision of your life and the work that you desire to do as the essence of you, as the soul of energy. Everything that you do, done from the energy of creativity, regardless of whether you are sweeping the floor, cleaning the toilets, washing the windows, washing the dishes, cooking the meal, writing the checks, creates a different possibility and a different result."
– Gary Douglas

Have you ever felt like Creativity is an elusive myth? *Totally-inaccessible-only-available-for-the-Greek-gods* type mythological? What if it is *that* intangible?

Have you ever considered the possibility? It seems frustrating, right? What if it didn't have to be that way? *This is what I'd like to invite you to in this chapter.*

Indulge me for a minute here, and read the opening quote again. How many intangible words are there in Gary Douglas's definition of Creativity?

Vision, Desire, Essence, Soul, Energy, Possibility…

Do you know exactly what those are? I don't! However, they all have an energy and energy is the source of all things.

But what if you don't 'get' energy?

My question is: **Is that really true?**

It sounds bizarre, have you ever been told you're an Infinite Being? Is that true and light for you? If so, would an infinite being not know energy?

Maybe English or the language you first spoke isn't your first language at all, what if energy is? Is that light for you?

Does this sound like gibberish already? I get it! And I wrote it to be this way! I'm not purposely trying to annoy you. I'd like to bring up the energy of everything that's currently in the way of you having and receiving The Energy of Creativity – **and change it.**

How does that sound to you?

I'm going to ask your brain to take a hike for this chapter and to read this from a non-linear perspective – go with the energy, wonder at the words in these pages and read this from a different point of view than you ever have before.

If your brain and way of thinking could figure out the energy of creativity – wouldn't you have done so already and be wildly creative in every area of your life?

Would you be willing to try something different, at least for the duration of this chapter? If you're not sure how, all you have to do is ask.

The Energy of Creativity

Yes? Let's go!

What is Creativity anyway?

> The dictionary says: creativity |krē-ā'tivitē|
> noun
> the use of the imagination or original ideas, especially in the production of an artistic work.

This is not the energy and joy I know creativity to be. Good thing we're screwing the rules in this chapter and going with a sense of wonderment and non-linearity! What really matters is what creativity is to you.

If you're the kind of person that loves writing notes and doing exercises – ponder for a moment **what is creativity to you?** (and write it down).

Your point of view creates your reality, and if this is the case, then the dictionary's point of view could be completely irrelevant if it doesn't match yours!

Knowing your own point of view can completely change the way you create and be (and the great thing is, if you don't like it, you can change it). What I find eliminates and stagnates creativity faster than anything is sticking fiercely to your point of view – especially if it's not working for you.

Is that light for you?

> *"When we start to stagnate, what we really need is a heavy dose of another fancy term: divergent thinking. Divergent thinking is what happens when your brain begins to imagine any possibility, head off in any direction and deliberately diverge from the conventional, looking for more options than*

what currently exists.

And do you know what happens then?

Your brain has a hey day. It begins to pulse back and forth between divergent thinking and convergent thinking, and starts to combine new information with old and forgotten ideas.

And do you know what the outcome is? A little thing called creativity.

That's actually the science behind creativity. And do you know what a little creative thinking leads to?

The "ah ha!" moment you've been waiting for. (Though unfortunately, that doesn't actually make a light bulb pop up above your head. And trust us—no one is more heartbroken about this than us.)"

~ Ash Ambridge, The Middle Finger Project

I'm not really interested in talking about the brain or the science behind creativity in this chapter, you can get plenty of wonderful studies and scientific information elsewhere by people more qualified. What I would like to have is a conversation on energy you may never of have before.

So how do you communicate the energy of it?! The last book Erica invited me to write in was *The Energy of Receiving* and when I started researching, I came across this quote:

"If you are unwilling to receive, you cannot be nurtured and you cannot nurture another, nor can you

have joy, creativity, or any of those other fun things. If you won't nurture and care for yourself, then you can't receive that from someone else."

~ Gary Douglas, Founder of Access Consciousness®

But what really is receiving? This is where it becomes fun to write – it's indefinable too! And luckily in my work and now my writing, I don't have to have the answer - only wonderment about the world. I wonder… what is receiving to you? I can spout off a billion different meanings, research, dictionary definitions and metaphors, but if it's not what resonates with you – is it relevant? A mentor to me said, *"Your point of view creates your reality."* If your point of view creates your reality, what is your point of view about receiving? (Are you seeing the repeating points yet?)

If your point of view creates your reality and you have a point of view about receiving that does not work for you, would you be able to receive? Have you ever had a moment (or many!) where joy, creativity and fun seem impossible? What if that wasn't because of some mythical and elusive 'reason'?

Is it possible it could be a choice? To receive or not receive? What if creativity could be as easy as that?

Here's the secret: It *is*.

If your point of view creates your reality, what kind of reality would you like to create? Creating of any kind is one of the most generative and joyful energies in my life – in fact if I'm personally not creating and having 20+ things on my plate all the time, my life starts to lose it's sheen and get slow.

How many creations going all the time is actually enough for you?

Are you a one thing at a time person?

Two? Three? Four?

What about 10? 15? 20?

Which number feels light to you? Is there one that has a ping? Or is it all of them above one!?

Nobody warned you before purchasing this book (or maybe someone did!) that I'm insane. I have a totally different point of view on creating and functioning. However, the more crazy, insane, intense and busy I get, the more I'm becoming a contribution and invitation for other people.

One thing I do know is true for me, is overwhelm is a farce. I'm currently working on four different businesses, a possible investment in Italy (as of yesterday!), a charity project and a travel schedule and I'm looking for more. What if you gave yourself permission to desire more? Not from a space of ingratitude for what you currently have, simply from the knowing that there is more possible you would like to see in the world. That type of viewpoint is what gradually changes the world.

This doesn't mean I have no moments of total overwhelm, losing it, breaking apart or not knowing where to start. We all have those. It's what you choose in the moment that creates a difference. The morning after I got back from my last big tour, I was contemplating how much I was not inspired by the multitude on my plate after 36 hours of travel and some intensive "no time for work" travel. When I'm not inspired, to-do lists weigh more than a mountain – can you relate?

The Energy of Creativity

So instead of cutting down my list or hiring it out I do something insane: **Ask for more.**

"What would I have to add today to change this right away?" was the question I asked. Then I moved on to looking at my emails and "Pop!" Erica Glessing pops into my inbox with a possibility of co-creating a program that exactly matches the energy of my earlier question.

That was all it took to pull me out from under my mountain and into the Energy of Creativity.

So what points of view do you have about creativity that are stagnating it?

Again, if you're writing notes and doing exercises you could write down these here!

Do any of those make you feel lighter or heavier?

What's true for you always makes you feel lighter, a lie for you will make you feel heavier. Even if it's true for someone else, it might not be true for you.

What if you didn't have to have those lies anymore? Would you be willing to let those go?

Ready for a different perspective?

Try on a few of these for size:

- Overwhelm is an invitation to be greater
- An infinite being would never choose to have a limit
- The only limit on what you can create is the limit you choose
- You have to be willing to ask for more

- Know you will always have the capacity to step up

I know this is a lot of information thrown at you at once, so let's play with these!

Overwhelm is an invitation to be greater.

As you may know now, I'm (at the very least!) slightly insane – to me overwhelm is the invitation to play games!

Imagine you have a dog that loves to play, has insatiable energy and you have a bucket full of balls. You start throwing them and he starts chasing all of them! He may not get to every single ball but he's aware of them all and picking up the ones that would be fun to chase!

Is the dog overwhelmed or excited?

Is it possible you have a much more similar way of functioning to the dog than to a normal human being?

To me overwhelm is like playing fetch - supercharged.

"Oooh there's so many great possibilities to play with – which is one do I want to play with right now? Then what next? And what next? How many can I play with right now? Can I expand that? Can I outcreate my current capacities?"

Would that make it easier to create? My easiest tool when I do get overwhelmed is to start asking questions. And if you want to play the insane game:

- What would it take for this amount of overwhelm to be my easiest bare minimum amount to play with?

- What would it take to outcreate myself so much that this feels like nothing?

The Energy of Creativity

- Is this overwhelm really true or even mine?
- What would it take to go beyond this?

An infinite being would never choose to have a limit.

Truly, as an infinite being would you *ever* have limitations, or would you try them on like dress-ups to 'pretend' to be as sad or unhappy, or have as many problems as everyone else? Now I know this sounds harsh, and I apologize if this offends you (bringing up the energy here!).

Just go with me here for a sec? Does it make you feel lighter? Maybe we're really good at buying our dress-ups as real-life clothes. Does it make you feel lighter that limitations are dress-ups you're trying on for size?

What if you let yourself be as wonderful, fabulous, unlimited and full of enormous amounts of possibility and unstoppable energy you truly be?

Would this be more fun?

All it takes is a choice if you'd like to have it be different. "*Is this really a limitation I have or a dress-up I'm pretending is real?*"

The only limit on what you can create is the limit you choose.

This goes hand and hand with my strong talk above – what point of view do you have about how much creativity and energy you can have? Is it really true that you have a limited amount?

Or is it more: *How much (more) are you willing to have?*

It could be intense, it could make you feel more alive than ever before or take you on a journey not many people are willing to go on – is what you have been asking for though?

There's this weird global point of view that it's better to be with people and miserable than go a journey alone and truly choose for you – **I'm calling bullshit!**

For what reason is it better to wallow with other people in the shit of combined misery (or if misery is too strong – complacency, just-getting-by, boredom or unhappiness) than have true happiness and a generative life beyond any adventure before?

How is it a contribution to the world to be as sad as everyone else?

- Does it change the sad people (if they're willing to change)?
- Does it inspire others to choose different?
- Does it make your life wonderful, amazing and an adventure beyond everything you've ever known?
- Does it make you happy?

Or does it bring you down, contract your being and stagnate everything in your life so much you feel like time is running backwards – not forwards?

The secret is: When you're willing to go the journey alone even if no one else can go with you, your true friends and people come into your universe.

You have to be willing to ask for more.

We live in a universe where *ask and you shall receive* actually works. The only thing that's required is for you to be willing to ask and receive.

What if it really is that easy? Would you be willing to play with this?

What could you ask for that you haven't been asking for because you think you might actually get it and that would shake up your world too much?

Is now the time? Are you over not having what you truly desire and know is possible?

I know I am, so why not ask? The worst answer is no and even then that can change. You won't know until you ask (and here's a hint – you're not asking other people, ask your entire being and the universe instead).

Know you will always have the capacity to step up.

Think back to where you were a year ago. Are you the same person you are today as then? What about 5 years ago? 10 years ago?

Or have you changed, grown, and gotten stronger than before?

Yes?

How cool is that!

As an infinite being, would you have the capacity to expand your strengths, talents and abilities?

How much fun can you have when your very being grows and expands with every choice you make? Does that sound like a fun reality to you?

If you'd like to have it – guess what?!

It's another choice you have available to choose. And if

you're wondering how you choose, great question!

A lot of people don't know how to choose. I'll let you in on a secret - I don't know how to choose either! For some reason I just do it, it's a weird capacity everyone has the ability to have that remains a total mystery. Do you know how to make your heart beat? I don't! I don't know how to choose either, what I do know is that my heart beats and I choose.

The reason I say that is because I'm a different person every day. Are you the same person you were a year ago, or what even about six months ago? Forget it, even one day ago! Just one day ago.

The secret to choice is you don't need to know how to do it. Do you know how to breathe or is it something you innately do? What if choice is actually as natural to you as breathing? Does that feel light to you? Would you be willing to play with it? Have fun even?

Just choose anything! There's no right or wrong in that. When you choose it, it gives you an awareness of "Oh, this is working for me. This isn't working for me. Ok, I'm going to play with this some more. I'm not going to play with this anymore." And that's that.

And if you come across a moment when you are really struggling with "I don't know how to choose," this is what I do. I ask, "How do I choose today?" or "What would choosing look like today?" Or I'll go outside and say "Ok, nature, ok universe, ok anyone, like I'm being real dumb today. What is choice? Show me choice." Anything that I'm not currently getting, I will generally go outside, and even to my cat, because I don't know how, but my cat's always choosing consciousness. And I'll ask, "Show me consciousness." Or "Show me choice." Or "Show me possibility." The thing is if you ask, you will receive. They will come to you. Ask and you shall receive actually works!

The other question I ask when I'm not getting something is "What would it take for me to get what choice is?" You don't actually have to know the answer to anything anymore. What if you just needed to be smart enough to ask a question? I'll hear someone say something and I'll sit there like a dog watching television and I'm going "I'm not getting this" and then the next moment I ask, "what would it take for me to get it?" It can be as simple as that.

I've often found that when I sit there like a dog watching television and I don't get something, it's because that's not my issue at all. So I look there and I'm like "oh I don't get this" but then it's not my stuff, that's why I don't get it. This is also something that I talk about with my mum when she gets so lost she says, "I don't get this. How did this take so long?" All it takes is for me to ask here "Well, when did you finish it or change it?" and then she goes "Oh, five seconds before you started talking about it." What if you were that fast too?

What else is possible now?

While this chapter doesn't talk a lot about my journey with creativity or the pragmatics of how this can show up, it opens a doorway to the possibilities that go much further than a "How-to" guide.

Questions are tools and points of view create your reality. As you explore what you would really like to have with the Energy of Creativity, asking questions, looking at your point of view, having wonderment about how you're functioning will change your reality more than anything else I could offer.

Intangible Insanity – A Different Source Point of Creativity

The only thing that's in your way of creativity is you.

Would you like to get out of your way?

Is now the time?

Our world is asking, begging and demanding a change - One where being on the creative edge, consciousness and being a change are the new valuable products. You being you is what's required and desired from the universe.

Are you willing to be it? All it takes is a choice.

Hint: The universe has your back and will help you to if you ever require it.

About the Author

REBECCA HULSE

Rebecca Hulse is a go-getting, risk-taking millenial. She is a #1 bestselling author, Benevolent Capitalist, creator of magnitude, International Speaker, Joy of Business® Certified Facilitator and Access Consciousness Certified Facilitator. Rebcca loved shaking up the supposed hard-set realities and paradigms kept in place over lifetimes.

She sees a different reality and possibility - usually far beyond this reality which she has used to create her own life and business traveling the world from New Zealand to Costa Rica, USA, Europe, Australia, the Caribbean and beyond.

She is the author of three books including The Energy of Receiving (her latest and 1st bestseller) and speaks to a global audience on business, leadership, consciousness, and more.

You can reach Rebecca at www.rebeccahulse.com and also receive a free judgment cleanse.

Chapter 3

CREATIVITY EXPONENTIALIZED: EXPLORING THE BIG PICTURE

By Meredith Locher

"Creativity is not just for artists. It's for business people looking for a new way to close a sale; it's for engineers trying to solve a problem; it's for parents who want their children to see the world in more than one way."

~ Twyla Tharp

There is little in life I love to talk about and play in more than the energy of creativity. I have realized recently that I have an understanding of creativity that is quite different.

The truth is creativity is an enigmatic concept with many definitions, many expressions, and a whole lot of misperceptions.

What is creativity anyway?

Is it art-related? For most people, the mind goes straight to the arts such as painting, writing, sculpting, acting, and dance.

Is it a talent or skill only "creative" people possess?

Is creativity something you have been avoiding since you've been unclear?

The definitions are endless. Here are just a few...

- Creativity is the act of turning new and imaginative ideas into reality.

- The use of the imagination or original ideas, especially in the production of an artistic work.

- The ability to transcend traditional ideas, rules, patterns, relationships, or the like, and to create meaningful new ideas, forms, methods, interpretations, etc.; originality, progressiveness, or imagination.

- The tendency to generate or recognize ideas, alternatives, or possibilities that may be useful in solving problems, communicating with others, and entertaining others and ourselves.

- 1828 definition - To produce; to bring into being from nothing; to cause to exist. To form anew; to change the state or character; to renew.

Compared to my awareness of what creativity really is, most of the definitions only serve to confine it rather than define it. The less confining, more general definitions such as the 1828 definition are actually the closest to what I know creativity to truly be.

What if everything you think you know about creativity is actually not true?

I so often hear people say, "I am just not a creative person." What if that is one of the biggest lies of all?

If you were to pull back from the limiting ideas and art connections, what could creativity be to you that you haven't ever realized or acknowledged?

Is creativity involved in the arts? Yes!

Is it occasionally related to creating a product? Yes!

Does an outcome have to be achieved or do you have to be engaging in an art form or creating a product to be playing in the energy of creativity? No!

So what is creativity really?

Creativity is an energy, an expression, ever-changing, ever-flowing that lives in us, through us, as us, and because of us.

Creativity is always in the question, never the conclusion. Curiosity is a key component of creativity.

Creativity is perfectly imperfect, always innovating and never complete.

I wonder? Where in your life are you expressing the energy of creativity? Where are you in the question? Where are you innovating?

Now, this is the really weird question…what if you have actually been creating every moment, every hour, every day throughout all time? What?! How can that be true?

What if you were created as a creator who lives and breathes creativity through every expression of you? And

Creativity Exponentialized: Exploring the Big Picture
Meredith Locher

what if YOU and your life are your own greatest creation?

To me, creativity is what creative people do. And creative people are people who were created by their creator to live life and this living life is THE most beautiful creation of all.

What if all of life and living is creativity? All of it. Not just the painting and writing, but the whole entire journey including the growing, the changing, the struggling, and the choosing!

Now, I realize some of you may have ease accepting this idea. Others may be able to both accept it and be conflicted about it at the same time. And then there are those of you who may have great difficulty grasping the concept that all of life, including you, is and has always been, creativity in action.

What do you know about creativity that you have never acknowledged?

Is it possible that creativity is an energy that is expressed in our every waking moment (and quite likely, even while we sleep)?

Is it possible that you are way more creative than you have ever acknowledged?

See, to me, it is clear that my every step and every choice and every breath is creative and this is one of the most delicious, fun truths about life!

What would life be if you treated it more like your creation? What would you change?

It is possible to just start now? Right now?

So starting now, look at your home…is there anything

you would like to create differently there? What will it take to create that?

You may find many ideas come to mind like…"I would like to paint my walls and add crown molding. I'd like to change the color scheme and make it more elegant. I would love a new sofa and I would definitely like it to be more organized."

You may also get clear awareness about how to go about making those changes such as, "I will look through pictures online to get the colors I would like then ask the person at the paint store to help me choose the closest colors. And I will ask my brother in-law who does some handy work to help with crown moldings, start saving for the new sofa, and create an organization plan that works with my schedule."

Or…you may be more like most people who either have no idea what they would like to change or have ideas, but all the reasons none of that is possible come straight to mind.

This is all part of creativity. Sometimes it flows and sometimes there are roadblocks. Those who are prolific in their creations simply keep choosing to create. They also keep asking questions and look for possibilities that will open the doors to new ideas and to bringing those ideas to fruition.

What else can you sprinkle creativity dust onto?

What about your work? Are you doing what you love? Are you making enough money? What innovation is possible there that you have not yet considered?

I so often find people feel trapped in their work. They decide or conclude something about it that keeps them locked in. Concluding is not creative. Beyond the conclusions and limitations and "becauses," what can you change with regard to your work? What can you add to your work life that will make all the difference right now? What can you choose now to create a future with work that is way more fun and rewarding?

What else?

Relationships? If you were truly creating your life, what would you change in your relationship? You can change "you" to "I" and ask that question about every person in your life…your partner if you have one, your family members, and your friends. What creativity is required or desired in all of these relationships?

We can often be dramatic and go straight to extremes, but just like the small, subtle strokes in a painting of the ocean that may express the ripples, there are actually small, subtle changes that can create a massive difference in your relationships. And you may also find that big changes are necessary. What changes big and small can you make in your relationships that would help you create the life you would like to live?

What about YOU?

What if you are one of the greatest creations now in the hands of you to innovate?

What if we are created exactly as we are meant to be… with everything our creator meant us to have so that we can have all the experiences we came here to have?

We were created. We are living, walking, talking expressions of creativity. Once created, you were handed off to your parents to make sure you, in your delicate, developing phase, were supported. Some parents sucked at this part and you had to start creating yourself and your life earlier than others. Some parents were great at this and that also effected how you created yourself and your life and a huge variety of ways. No matter what though, and in spite of what most parents would lead us to believe, you have always been yours and your life has always been yours to create.

> *"There is only one of you in all time, this expression is unique. And if you block it, it will never exist through any other medium and it will be lost."*
>
> ~ Martha Graham

What creativity are you expressing as you now?

What, if anything, would you like to innovate in you?

Now, this is a huge possibility for creativity that most people ignore or undervalue. There really is only one you. You have infinite capacities whether you know it or not. You have infinite possibilities for change. You have infinite expressions in spite of the definitions you may have of you. You are an expression of the infinite and you are perfectly imperfect, always innovating and never complete.

I know you probably think there is more about you that you can't change than you can. Yet the fresh, new inventions we enjoy every day were born by someone who was unwilling to believe what existed before was all that was possible. The new song, new play, new book, new technology all came from people who knew change was possible and gave it a go.

> *"Around here, however, we don't look backwards for very long. We keep moving forward, opening*

up new doors and doing new things, because we're curious...and curiosity keeps leading us down new paths."

~ *Walt Disney*

What would you be willing to be curious about with regard to you? What have you concluded you are that you are not? What can you change about you that you have never acknowledged is possible?

For most people, this list can be long. And that's okay. We have all completed things we didn't think we could and we have all had the experience of something taking far less time than it seemed like it would.

Would you be willing to create you? Would you be willing to innovate even the conclusion that you can't? What if you could be your own greatest expression of creativity? If you were truly creating you, where would you start? If you were creating you like a work of art, would you treat yourself differently than you have been?

We are not supposed to be done. We are not supposed to be perfect. We are creativity and energy, an expression, ever changing, ever flowing that lives in us, through us, as us, and creativity exists because of us.

Imagine what this world would be like if everyone was embracing the creator they are and willing to choose to innovate what isn't working.

What expression of creativity are you that if you were to embrace it, and share it, would change your reality and maybe even change the world?

"Creativity is contagious, pass it on."
~ *Albert Einstein*

About the Author

MEREDITH LOCHER, MA, CH

Meredith Locher, MA, CH, is a creator extraordinaire, constantly recreating and out-creating herself in every area of life. She is an author, speaker, Transformational Coach, Master Hypnotherapist, and Energetic Change Agent. Meredith empowers clients to find their way, their truths, and to create their lives in a way that not only works for them, but also makes them happy!

For the past 16 years, Meredith has been guiding people to resolve every imaginable challenge including anxiety, depression, insecurities, phobias, relationship & sexual dysfunction, substance abuse, eating disorders, physical pain, chronic diseases, infertility, business & financial challenges, athletic & artistic blocks and so much more. She approaches every client with kindness, caring, and from a space of no judgment. If she could create anything in this world, it would be more spaces of non-judgment, and more consciousness on the planet. She often asks questions like, "What would be possible if you stopped judging you?"

Meredith sees clients internationally via Skype & phone as well as locally in-person in multiple locations in Southern California.

Look for more books coming soon from Meredith! To connect with Meredith, visit: YourPathCoach.com

Chapter 4

THE POWER OF WORDS TO CREATE

By Megan Walrod

Do you believe that creativity is just for artists and sculptors?

What if I told you that you don't need paint or clay to be creative?

What if life is the medium through which you create?

The truth is we are all capable of high levels of creativity.

We are each given the invitation to create our lives.

And the one medium we all use to create our lives?

WORDS

The words we use to describe who we are and what we do determine everything about our lives. As the famous 14th century Sufi poet said:

> *"The words you speak become the house you live in."*
>
> *~ Hafiz*

What kind of "house" or life are you creating?

Are you using words that inspire and create or words that hurt and destroy?

> *"Words can inspire. And words can destroy. Choose yours well."*
> *~ Robin Sharma*

Here are some examples of the different kinds of words you might be using to create (or destroy) your own life:

Example A:
Life happens to me. I never have enough. Everyone is out to get me. I'm overwhelmed. I'm stuck. I don't know what to do.

Example B:
Life is an adventure that I create every day. I always have what I desire. I have more than enough of everything. The world is conspiring to support my joy and success. I'm inspired. I'm inspiring. I live in possibilities.

> *"What you think you become."*
> *~Buddha*

Have you ever used the words in Example A to create your life?

I have. These kinds of words did more to destroy my life. Although at the time I was using them, my life already felt destroyed.

I was navigating a divorce and feeling overwhelmed by big waves of anger, grief, betrayal and abandonment. "How could this have happened to me?" I wondered. "How could he do this to me?" I blamed. "Nobody sees how wrong this is." I fumed.

I suffered immensely as I shot words at myself and my ex-husband, proving to myself that I was a helpless innocent, victim to someone else's actions.

**What helped me shift from using words that destroyed
to words that create?**

I used the tools and resources I'm about to share with you to heal and transform. In the process, I stopped seeing myself as a victim and started to become the heroine of my own life.

Now I coach women entrepreneurs around the world on what words to use to inspire and empower themselves and their ideal clients. I've grown a successful business guiding other women on how to create success for themselves.

So how can you make the shift from words that destroy to words that create?

The first step to creating any kind of change is to acknowledge where you are right now.

If you've been using words like those I shared in Example A to create (or destroy) your life, I have good news: the tools and resources in this chapter will guide you on how to use new words to create your life and the success you desire.

If you've been using words like those I shared in Example B, congratulations! By using words that empower and inspire, you set yourself up for success. You can also use the tools and resources in this chapter to amplify the beauty and possibilities you're already creating in your life.

"Change your thinking, change your life!

Your thoughts create your reality."
~ Les Brown

The Healing Power of Journaling

Journaling was a lifeline during my divorce, as well as at other difficult times in my life.

I found solace in the blank pages that became my witness and companion during times when I felt lost and alone. Allowing my grief, anguish, anger and angst to wash through me and flow out onto the pages was healing.

And I let it all spew forth from me onto the page. Words of anger and hatred. Questions of "Why me?" Tears of loss.

I fully surrendered into feeling disempowered. I felt small and invisible. I felt like the pain would never end. I felt like the world was against me.

One night it all shifted. I was angry. I was slapping thick layers of red and black paint onto a large canvas. All the words I'd been using to describe this story that kept me powerless exhausted themselves. I found a new word:

ENOUGH

I stormed through the house saying it over and over again, "Enough. Enough. Enough! Enough! ENOUGH!"

As my anger burned its way through me I recognized I had a role to play in my divorce. I had created this. I decided I was going to do everything I could to never again repeat this experience.

This decision birthed a new set of words in the form of the question, "What role did I play in my divorce?"

The Energy of Creativity

I began to create a new "house" for myself (as Hafiz said) and started to explore other questions in my journaling:

- What is the pattern I am playing out with my ex-husband?
- How is this pattern familiar?
- How does this reflect my relationship with the Masculine?
- What can I do to change this and create a new relationship with the Masculine (and myself)?
- What new life do I wish to create for myself?

I also started to describe myself in new ways: I am the heroine of my own life. I am strong. I am courageous. I am powerful. I am resilient. I am creative.

> *"You can't stop the waves,*
> *but you can learn how to surf."*
> *~ Jon Kabat-Zinn*

I no longer felt overwhelmed by the waves I was navigating. I learned how to "surf," and ride the waves of grief and change to create a new life for myself.

What Is the Gift of Journaling?

Being able to capture my experience through my divorce (and beyond) in words helped me make sense and ultimately make meaning out of the nonsensical. Writing – and the words I used to describe my journey – helped me understand the journey I was choosing, harvest the gifts and plant seeds for new growth.

As I gave voice to all of my many parts and perspectives (the victim, the heroine, the one who sees the wrongness in a situation, the one who sees the rightness), I unleashed my full voice without inhibitions. This opened the way to being more authentic and expressive in my life beyond my journal.

I also tapped into my inner voice that showed me how to create a new, inspiring and empowering life for myself. This inner voice became my guiding light.

I'm sharing the tool of journaling with you so you can tap into your own guiding light and the words that will create your most inspiring life.

> *"As we write, we are both describing and deciding the direction that our life is taking."*
> *~ Julia Cameron*

Journaling Can Be A Journey Of:

- **Inquiring**: getting curious about your own experiences, choices, beliefs, behaviors and possibilities

- **Reflecting**: seeing your situation from other perspectives and making sense and meaning from your experience

- **Cultivating**: trusting yourself to listen to all parts of yourself and strengthening your ability to tune into your inner guidance

- **Unlocking:** sharing all the silences and secrets you held in for so long

- **Unleashing:** releasing all of you to be seen, heard, felt and expressed

Whether you have never journaled before or have been journaling since you were a child, here are some tips to guide you in making the most out of this creation tool.

Top 10 Tips on Journaling

The intention of journaling is to write without inhibitions. To allow all that is flowing through you to be released onto the page freely.

Use these simple guidelines to create a safe, inspiring space to journal.

1. Set aside a distraction-free quiet space for you to write. (While I have written in noisy cafes and on buses and airplanes, I've found that quiet space is very conducive to fully engaging with my inner voice.)

2. Put your pen to the paper or fingers to the keyboard and write, allowing anything and everything to come forward. Don't try to figure it out or plan what you are going to say. This is considered stream-of-consciousness writing: let it all out as it arises.

3. Do not edit yourself as you write. Grammar mistakes and typos are welcome.

4. Do not censor what wants to come forth onto the page. Allow it all: the good, the bad and the ugly.

5. As much as possible, do not judge what you write.

6. Do let all inner voices be heard.

7. Do allow yourself to be surprised.

8. You can pause, reflect and re-read what you've written but don't reorganize or re-write what you've written.

9. If you reach a place where you feel "blocked" with your writing yet feel the desire to keep writing, use the "writing prompts" below or keep writing the same line over and over again until something shifts and more comes through.

10. Be willing to experiment: if you always write in the morning in your lined journal, see what it's like to write in the evening on blank sheets of paper or in a word document on your laptop (and vice versa).

Another Tool: Writing Prompts

Writing prompts are a useful tool to spark your creativity and give you inspiration if you're not quite sure where to start with your writing. They can also be used to access new perspectives and possibilities through your writing.

Here's how you use them:

1. Pick a prompt.//
2. Write in a stream-of-consciousness style for 5-15 minutes with one prompt.
3. Do not edit or revise as you write. As Nathalie Goldberg says (author of *Writing Down The Bones)*, "Put your pen to the paper and go." No stopping.
4. Your writing doesn't need to remain directly connected to the original prompt. Free-form expression is what you're going for here.

Fun and Frivolous Prompts

Here's a list of prompts you can use that are fun and may

The Energy of Creativity

even seem frivolous. Yet they are intended to awaken more of your imagination and creativity.

1. I wrap my purple cape around my shoulders and…
2. As I walk along the dirt path I notice…
3. I look out the window and am surprised to see…
4. The sunlight dances on the water and reminds me of…
5. The little girl wore a tutu and butterfly wings…
6. A loud sound startles me and as I turn around…
7. I open up the treasure chest and out pours…

Unlocking and Unleashing Prompts

Here is another kind of writing prompt. These invite you to unleash other layers of yourself you may not have been aware of till now:

1. One thing I wouldn't want you to know about me is…
2. Sometimes I feel…
3. The words that describe my light are…
4. The words that describe my shadow are…
5. The words that describe who I am becoming are…
6. I really desire…
7. I choose to create…

Be The Creator You Are

Journaling and writing prompts are two (of many) tools you can use to create your life. And the beauty of these tools is they encourage you to play and experiment. There is no one right way to use these. And there is definitely not a wrong way to use them.

So will you give yourself permission to unleash all those words you've been carrying around inside onto a blank page?

You are an artist:
Create your life
With words that
Inspire and empower.

About the Author

MEGAN WALROD, MA

Megan Walrod, Founder of Live Your Yes, LLC, is a copywriting and business coach, writer and #1 bestselling author. She shows savvy women entrepreneurs how to create marketing materials that are authentic and lucrative.

Megan has coached hundreds of entrepreneurs, supporting them to grow their business to 6-figures while living their purpose. She was one of the lead coaches, trainers and copywriters for a premier 7-figure company in the marketing industry. Before that, she was a consultant for a Global Fortune 500 Company, writing and delivering training for an international audience.

She received a Master's degree in Organization Development (from Bowling Green State University) and one in Transpersonal Counseling Psychology (from Naropa University). Her love of learning is surpassed only by her love of words, and showing her clients how to use them to inspire and empower.

Megan encourages her clients to "Live Your Yes," knowing that when we live an inspired life, we are more magnetic and create greater success for everyone. She's passionate about working with women entrepreneurs, as she knows that their success leads to greater consciousness, kindness and sustainability on our beautiful planet.

A big believer in "paying it forward," Megan contributes to organizations like Kiva.org (who provide micro-loans to entrepreneurs around the world) and the Unstoppable Foundation (who provide education and more for children in Africa).

Megan loves journaling and laying on the earth, as well as the smell and whisper of the ocean, and the hint of magic beneath the surface of every wave and word.

Chapter 5

MAGIC OF CREATIVITY

By Katherine McIntosh

Picture this: You are 8 years old and love the idea of dreaming and visioning. You have tea parties with imaginary friends, or tag football or wrestling with imaginary friends. You play trains, dream of being an actress, model, pro-athlete, wrestler, and a myriad of other feats. You dream of all the things you want to do…. play, go to Disneyland, ride in a hot air balloon, win a gold medal in the winter Olympics….and the summer Olympics, become a professional football player, or soccer player, or basketball player. You play with sand castles and swim in the ocean, and ride on the beach, and dive, and swim, and ride bikes, and ski, and travel, and….the list goes on and on.

If you are like most 8 year olds (or any child for that matter), you have an extraordinary imagination. You love to play, and paint, and play, and play, and make up dance moves, and dream about sports, and in your world, the idea of getting paid for BEING you is just part of the genetic makeup of being an extraordinary, magical creature that uses the joy of your body and mind to visualize the possibilities that you have yet to discover.

And then you get older, and adults start asking you the

proverbial question:

What do you want to do when you grow up?

It's like that question is *supposed* to inspire greatness…so you start dreaming about all the things you could potentially "DO" to get paid for being a grown up… It's like the list is endless and has magic and money written all over it. However, as you share your dreams, your magic…you want to play basketball, be a doctor, lawyer, musician, teacher, create a famous app that makes you wealthy, and travel the world, and…

And all of the sudden you look at the questioning adult and see that your list of magical possibilities does not exist in their universe….

"Those are nice dreams, but what about the REAL world?"

The REAL world? Is the real world one that smashes dreams, and tells you to get practical as if being practical was the window into happiness? Have you looked around you lately? How many adults do you know love their job, are happy in their relationships, make tons of money, have freedom of choice, and are willingly inspired to dream with you?

As a kid, I was a dreamer, a magical, inspired, creative dreamer. I loved to play sports and be active, and spend hours talking to my imaginary friends in the closet (who weren't actually so imaginary). I used stuffed dolls to have my strict Irish Catholic Parents believe I was talking to stuffed animals and stuffed dolls instead of revealing to them, the real secret…

I was having lots of conversations with lots of different

The Energy of Creativity

energies whom just so happened not to have physical bodies.

I wanted to be somebody.

I wanted to be a famous soccer player, and win the gold medal for the women's Giant Slalom. I wanted to compete on the Women's Olympic Volleyball Team. I was obsessed with the idea that someday I was going to be somebody. I would be on TV, maybe an actress in an award winning TV show or a dancer for Madonna, or Prince, or even better than that, George Michel. It was going to happen….I was going to MAKE IT happen!

And then I turned 17 and I had to start thinking about college. My grades were those of a barely surviving academic C student. "Katherine's a fabulous kid, but her results in school are just satisfactory." For me, that was ok. I didn't really care about the academic portion of school… but put me in gym class and challenge me to run the fastest mile, or hold the women's record for longest standing arm hang or most pull ups or push ups done by a girl and I was her.

My senior year in High School I still held the record for 7th and 8th grade women's pull ups and standing arm hang, where you hold your body at a pushup with your chin above the bar and see for how long you can "hang" there. I think I got close to 3:00 minutes and no one in grade school had come close to budging the record.

I was scouted by top coaches in my area for softball, soccer, and volleyball. I lettered in Varsity all four years for soccer and three years for volleyball.

What the hell does all of this have to do with creativity?

The Magic of Creativity — Katherine McIntosh

I wanted to be someone and when I turned 17 I had to figure out what I wanted to BE when I grew up. It killed my creativity. I was going to college…where was I going? Would I play sports? Would I get a scholarship? What career path was I going to pick?

Career Path? I didn't even like studying!! How the hell was an athlete dreamer suppose to pick an academically oriented career at the age of 17 as if I was supposed to know what I wanted my life to look like outside of getting paid for being an athlete.

Fast-forward a year later and I am about to start playing soccer for a women's team in college and I had moved far away from the great Midwest. My mentality…the farther away from home the better (we'll save that for another story).

My parents, god bless their hard working deep seeded values, instilled in me that in order to get ahead in life, you had to be practical, willing to work your ass off, be polite, say please and thank you, and you can forget about getting paid to be a professional athlete.

Once I got to college and stepped on the practice field, the coach looked at me and said: "You better be ready to eat, breathe, and sleep soccer for the next four years." She was intense (that's putting it mildly) and she scared the crap out of me. I looked at her and then I looked at the mountains and started dreaming about rafting, and hiking, and skiing, and backpacking, and mountain biking, and…… I was supposed to put my life and playful self on hold to be slave to a woman I'm not sure I was convinced I liked very much. So I strong talked myself and walked away from eating, breathing, and sleeping soccer.

When I jumped off the soccer field, I jumped on the

The Energy of Creativity

dance floor and my BODY fell in love with DANCE!!

I was enrolled as a general studies major since I was at a Liberal Arts School, you could literally get a degree in Liberal Arts....yeah that's practical!! HA HA!! My parents loved that one! In one semester I fell in love with dance. I was hooked.....the only challenge was how the heck was I going to have a conversation with my parents about my new found love and self declared dance major? I was going to spend $80,000 on a DANCE MAJOR?

Yeah, that didn't go so well. So I spent the next two years flailing, struggling, pondering, questioning, rolling around in my head the proverbial question....What do I want to do when I grow up?

The problem is that nothing that I wanted to do matched the practical, make money, be responsible roles my parents wanted to fit me into. So what was a girl to do...?

Long story short, I went on a 20 year track record of changing my mind as to what I wanted to do.

WHY? Because no one bothered to mention creativity as a strength of character and longevity in happiness!

So, this un-practical, would rather dance and play character majored in Spanish Literature, traveled the world, back packed through South America, and skied in the mountains. For paid jobs I put myself through college by waiting tables, ski instructing, and doing everything I could think of on the side to make money. I was a hustler.

I taught Business English in Quito, Ecuador, South America, and translated documents for IBM South America. I landscaped, waited tables, was a barista, catered events, taught dance classes, was a personal assistant, ran a $60 Million/year Real Estate Business, became a high end

Licensed Real Estate Agent, was an Administrative Assistant, a nanny, a bartender, a dance teacher, a Somatic Psychotherapist, a glorified telemarketer, a caddy, a sales rep for Mary Kay and a myriad of other alternative income stream companies. I was an administrator for a Shamanic Teacher and followed him around the world taking classes and organizing his events. I started doing my own Shamanic Events, facilitating TranceDance and any other alternative modality I could think of. I've also been a HairStylist and an administrator for a yoga/dance/healing center. I worked on the Big Island of Hawaii as a prep chef and I'm sure have fit in other things I haven't even thought of including being a MOM.

Here's the thing: after I got over my athletic dreams simply existing as a vision that blissed my body out, I started to look at what I actually wanted to DO when I grew up...

I wanted to make a minimum of 6 figures healing bodies, teaching dance, doing alternative modes of healing, writing, and being. However, due to my "practical" background, there were ZERO examples of people that I knew of making 6 figures in alternative modes of healing.

So I worked for a Real Estate Company, wore a suit, and worked on bodies on the side. When I got sick enough to stop the round robin of never feeling like myself, I packed my bags and moved to Colorado to get a Masters Degree in Somatic Psychology. I had figured it out! I was going to earn a Masters and have a legitimate degree so I could work on people.

Long story short, that path didn't work out. It wasn't for me. I dropped out after my 1st year of a 3 year degree. And I am so glad I did. 10 years later after dropping out, most of my colleagues are only making $30,000 a year working in schools and hospitals and as struggling self-employed therapists and still have close to an $80,000 student loan. YIKES!

Is that creativity? Or does that kill the creative process? Bill Gates, Steve Jobs, and a myriad of other geniuses never finished college. They created a dream beyond what people could comprehend.

Creativity is the magic inside of you that is waiting for you to bring your visions to fruition for the world to see.

If you have a vision, then you also have all of the resources inside of you to make that vision or dream come to fruition. Creativity requires not looking for validation outside of you. It also requires doing whatever it takes and NEVER giving up.

I remember when I finally started doing things in my career that lit me up…I was 3 years into being a self-employed hairstylist for a high end salon in Boulder, Colorado. The owner said she had never seen someone fresh out of school build a loyal clientele so quickly. My mom, seeing my happiness remarked how creative she always knew I was.

It was like…HELLO! You're telling me this NOW! I'm 35 years old, had spent the good portion of my adult hood lost because she told me I had to be practical and now she was acknowledging my creativity! It was an aha moment. I loved hairstyling. I got to massage heads, make people feel better, and listen to their stories. I wasn't just a hairstylist, I was healing them, giving them hope, and I was also hearing things they would never tell their therapist.

Shortly after my mom made that comment, I no longer looked to her for validation and I started truly, outwardly pursuing my passion to make a bigger impact on the planet. I wanted to help people see that there was nothing wrong with them. I wanted to show them at their core they were creative, magic, and could do anything. I wanted to show them it was possible for them to embody the phenomenance and brilliance of their being with their creativity intact and fully engaged!

This reality is scared of making a living being creative. An artist, a musician, a songwriter. The competition is stiff and most practical people believe it's close to an impossible feat to become successful in the creative arts. A rare opportunity that only the lucky can afford. Most people, when they start something end up contracting their energy when they force themselves to be creative. Ask anyone who knows they have a book in them and then when they actually go to write it the fear, doubt, and distractions set in. How many people do you know that say....someday I'll write a book?

My response is always....why not now?

Creativity requires a fierce amount of determination as well as the belief in one self that it's actually possible. Whenever you look for validation from others, then you stifle the creative process and allow doubt and judgment to fester.

When you stop requiring validation from anything or anyone (including yourself) then you start to create the future of a different possibility and you start to be the invitation for others to choose the future of a different possibility.

If you can dream it, then you can do it! -Walt Disney

The Energy of Creativity

Walt Disney certainly knew the magic of creativity. Creativity inspires. The world needs more magic. The world needs you to be all of you!!

Does creativity liked to be calculated and controlled? NO! The whole point is to enjoy the journey. Look at Jackson Pollack; his paintings were not created from definition. Part of his genius is that there is no logical explanation as to the depth and breadth of what was in his mind when he was creating his masterpieces.

For me, creativity is when possibility meets space, meets the alchemy of you and what you know that no one else knows. It creates something that came together as if by magic. It's like going on an adventure and you don't quite know the end destination or what you will find along the way. The possibilities and the alchemy exist in the adventure and in not knowing.

For me, creativity is about playing with the molecules of space. Just like all the colors and palettes of a paintbrush that come together to create a masterpiece. Granted, some are better than others, but the point is, inside of you is some magical creation that no one else on the planet can create.

Are you listening?

Are you willing to listen to the whispers that give you butterflies in your stomach, that allow you to do what you would do all day long for FREE? What is that thing? What do you have inside you that the world is waiting for?

A book, a song, a poem, a lyric, a painting, a modality, a way of thinking, a new app, a new product, an idea, an image, a smile, a laugh. There is something in you that is worth a million dollars (at least).

When an idea comes in, pay attention to it, give it energy, ask it a question. If that idea came to you, there was a reason. You can do something about it. You can ask if this is for now or for the future. I use my phone and every time an idea comes through, I write it down. Sometimes I miss them and if they seem really amazing, I ask them to come back to me when I can write them down.

Creativity Requires S-P-A-C-E

Have you ever tried to write or read a book when someone is over your shoulder? Or have a deep conversation with someone when someone else is trying to eavesdrop? Does that kill the magic? Or make you want to write like crazy?

Creations like to have space to be able to allow the voice of what's being created to come through. Some may call it divine intervention, channeling, God Source, Buddha, whatever you call it; it is that thing that feels greater than just you. My point of view is that it IS YOU, when you are void of distraction and living in the space of possibility.

I talk about possibility a lot....

Creativity cannot exist without possibility. Possibility is the hope and dream that there is something greater out there. I would hope you think that as well. If not, why are you here? What are you here to do?

Me, I'm here to change the world by showing people their magic, unraveling the hidden gems inside of them that were waiting to be let out.

Creativity truly is a communion where you become one with space, the universe, the molecules of the universe and the tangible ability to bring something into existence that wasn't yet there before. To not be in the creative force and magic of your being, you have to separate you from you.

If you're not feeling creative or you have been experiencing a dry spell, then it might be time to ask to stop separating yourself from you, from others, from the earth, or anything else for that matter.

Consciousness includes everything and judges nothing.

We all have bad days, bad moments, challenges, that doesn't mean you aren't magical. It just means you need to get back to feeling in communion with all the molecules of the universe. Creativity is begging for you to actualize your dreams. If you have a dream inside you, then you DO have the knowing to do what it takes to actualize that dream into this reality. If it exists in your mind, it can exist in the world.

The problem is that most people do not believe fully in their ideas. They are waiting to see what they see out in tangible form to prove that it's possible. But if it's in your head…it's possible.

Have you always been creative? Have you always known there was another way to live life? Well, if you can follow the dreams inside of you, then this journey called life is waiting to take you on the adventure of your genius! Is now the time?

For me, when I found me, I was able to trust what I knew inside of me. I couldn't follow anyone else's formula or business plan. It either didn't work, or I got bored. Creativity is not boring; it creates endless possibilities for entertainment, amusement, pondering, questioning, and possibility.

If you are wondering how to bring out your creativity, find something that just lights you up, that brings every cell of your body to life. Find something that brings you JOY and do it and do it a lot. And then add questions to your daily life so you can begin to acknowledge the energy that comes forward.

It isn't about finding the answer, it's about the ENERGY! The magic in a question is that it takes listening, listening to the subtle differences in the energy to ride the wave of possibilities. It is about being on the adventure to bring to fruition the match of energy that's in your head and heart.

When you begin to acknowledge that you will never have answers, only questions - that will lead to more energy and open up more doors to a future you can only begin to imagine. The key in the question is to ASK from curiosity. From that child who knows that it can be anything and anyone at anytime. That 8 year that had no limits on what he or she knew was possible.

If you are over 18, then now, more than ever is the time to bring back curiosity and questions into everything you do. If you truly will begin to allow yourself the joy and adventure of the journey, what shows up will surprise you and your life will unfold in ways that will bring tears to your eyes.

If you're wondering where to start, I always say, start with the question. Here is a list of a few of my favorites that have taken this stressed out, over worked pregnant hairstylist to an International Speaker and Facilitator traveling the world with ease and joy, a multi-6 figure business, all with a 2.5 year old. If I can do it, so can you. Embrace your creativity, lighten up, and begin to see yourself as the bright-eyed magical child you always knew you could be!

What can I create here and what will be fun for me?

What can I create today?

What adventure and possibility awaits me today?

What else is possible?

What can I create today that will out create my money flows right away?

What can I create today that will show me the magic of the universe?

Make a list of questions you can ask.... and remember, no question, if truly asked as a question is a wrong question to ask! Keep on playing your tune, the world is waiting to see your genius in action! It's time my friends, who's with me?

About the Author

KATHERINE MCINTOSH

Katherine McIntosh is an international speaker and facilitator on the topics of wealth, health, business, body, and living a vibrant lifestyle. She is a Business Wizard and Body Magician who has helped thousands of people monetize and value their genius, including actors, musicians, and 6 and 7 figure business owners. Katherine wrote the forward for the #1 best seller called The Energy of Expansion, and is a bestselling author for The Energy of Healing and I'm Having It! She is the CEO of Conscious Apple and the founder of the No Judgment Diet™, an international 30-day program that has helped hundreds of people get out of judgment with their bodies to create the business and life they love. She is a master at diving into the secret spaces of your life so that you can be your BEST self and take you, your body, your life, and your business to the next level of play & magic.

Katherine has traveled the world and worked with coaches, musicians, actors, and business owners making a difference on the planet. With a tenacious entrepreneurial spirit, Katherine has built multiple businesses from the ground up to amazing success in a short amount of time. Katherine is on a mission to change the way people see themselves, their bodies, food, their relationships and their creative capacities. Katherine believes that if you have a dream, then you have all the details inside of you to bring that dream to fruition. And no one else can actualize that dream in the same way you can. She is an Access Consciousness Certified Facilitator, a Motivational Speaker, Mom, and bestselling author who desires to show everyone their best and most brilliant selves! Are you ready for something different? It's time to let your magic shine!

Visit www.katherinemcintosh.com/freegift or www.nojudgmentdiet.com.

Chapter 6

Unlock Your Creativity, Unlock Your Emotions

By Laura Hackel

When you think about the word creativity, what words or images come up for you?

I find that I mostly think of the fine arts of painting and sculpting, or those cute and clever cupcakes you see on the covers of the magazines in the supermarket before every holiday. I know that my husband is a connector of people and he creatively sees connections between two people or businesses that they may not yet see themselves. I also resonate with the idea that sometimes you just need to get creative with your schedule so you can fit everything in or get each child to where they are supposed to be on a certain day.

What I realized over the summer is that I had also associated the word "perfect" with creativity. Like there is a "right" way to be creative. In other words, be creative as long as you stay in the box! Talk about two opposing forces. I want to share with you how I noticed this so you can see what you can notice for yourself.

It all started this past spring when we (collectively) made the decision that my 14-year-old daughter would be attending a boarding high school 90 minutes from our house. This was a "growth opportunity" for me on so many fronts as she's my youngest child (my two boys moved out several years ago) and my only daughter.

Now I knew that we are going to have to get creative in staying connected with her even while she's not living with us, but I had no idea about how creativity was about to rock my world (in a good way).

A little background, my daughter and I have been collecting her favorite outfits ever since she was a baby. Each time she outgrows something we have the discussion about whether it will be donated or put into bin for "The Quilt." On rainy afternoons I have found her rummaging through the bin that has all of the "quilt clothes" and we would share memories about a particular outfit or two.

You see, when I first had this idea over 18 years ago, I planned to send each one of my kids off to college with their "quilt." Somehow, life got busy and the boys escaped that fate (for now).

So in June, my daughter looks at me and innocently asks, "So that quilt, will it be ready in September?"

Of course I go into full on panic mode as my first thought is "I thought I had 4 more years to figure this out," and, "No way, I don't even know how to quilt!" What I say to her is "Of course it will be ready, honey." And then I start searching the Internet for articles, pictures and videos on how to quilt.

At this point I should tell you that not only do I not know how to quilt, but I have no distinctions for straight lines, something most quilts rely heavily upon. So, I do some research and decide a "crazy quilt" is my best choice. Now I know that I still need to problem solve how to get straight squares and I decide to order 10x10 inch muslin backing squares that are already cut and have straight edges.

So the beautifully straight squares arrive at my doorstep and I get everything out and follow step by step instructions on the first couple of squares until I get the hang of things. At this point I do the calculation that I need 60 more of these squares to make the quilt the size I want and that's when my creativity comes rushing in! I start playing with designs from my mind. A melding of colors and textures and memories all woven together. I literally decided that I have so many to do that it won't matter if some of them aren't "perfect."

At one point, I even cut one of her favorite Sherpa hats in half and top stitched it down onto an old pair of velour pants.

Now I am really on fire because I have given up my attachment to it being someone else's definition of perfect and I can stand in my own vision of it being full of love and light to wrap her in each night she's away so she knows and remembers and can feel how much I love her.

In my tight timeframe, I find that I am packing up my sewing machine and the quilting bin including the iron and rotary cutter (something I didn't even know existed weeks before) and putting them in the car whenever I go away for a few days. I found a way to get a few squares done every day.

And, as will happen when you are in creative flow, everything I needed showed up for me just when I needed it, from the rotary cutter to blanket binding ribbon. My daughter got in on the action too as I laid out all 63 squares and she helped me make sure all kittens (from pajamas she wore when she was three years old) were facing the right way, that the color was distributed pleasingly and that squares that were meant to be next to each other were.

Here's a picture of her one day as I caught her "rolling around" on her yet to be assembled quilt!

At the same time I was on my quilt-making journey I also:

- Broke one of my toes and then proceeded to bang it into everything else.
- Severely pulled my hamstring muscle on one of my legs and
- Generally experienced feet and leg pain.

So I asked myself "What's that all about"?

The Energy of Creativity

I know that feet and legs represent forward motion in the energetic world. My logical mind said there is forward motion everywhere; we are getting ready to send my daughter off and change is everywhere.

So, I asked an energy healer friend of mine what she saw going on. It may not surprise you (though it was a surprise to me), what she saw was my daughter and her upcoming move.

And that's when it hit me; I wasn't processing my emotions about how I felt about this upcoming life event. I kept telling myself that everything will be okay (and I know if will), but I also didn't allow myself the space to mourn the four more years that I thought I would have with her, or my fear that our close connection might suffer or the loss of what has always been a source of unconditional love for me.

No mistake here that our second chakra, (the space right below your belly button) is the source of all creativity AND emotions, feelings, intimacy and connection. So working on the quilt was both letting out my feelings and emotions and, because I wasn't processing them, I literally couldn't move forward.

What I noticed is that my toe and hamstring would hurt worse while I was working on the quilt until I chose to use quilting as a way for me to process this major change and to shift out of the mode of ignoring my feelings to being able to feel them and just sit with it so that I could move through them instead of blocking them.

It isn't a mistake that the more I let go of my worry and fear, the more fun the quilt was and the more permission I gave myself to color outside the lines. Yes, my daughter's quilt has a non-traditional fuzzy fleece backing and silky, satin blanket binding, because that's what is perfect for her.

Here are the lessons that making this quilt for my daughter taught me about creativity:

Just start. Right now, with what you already have. Try something, be willing to experiment and fail.

Be more attached to what you feel than the outcome. Allow yourself the freedom to explore and really tune into what you know deep in your heart even if you're not sure why

If you are feeling "blocked," check in with your second chakra. Guilt, people pleasing, perfection and concern about what others my think or say are all limiters of our creativity. To release blocks, move your body around and dance. Adopt a great second chakra affirmation like "I am open to experience the present moment with all my senses." For more affirmation and ideas check out www.chakra-anatomy.com.

Emotions and feelings might come up for you. You might experience body pain, and that's okay, pay attention to where you are feeling it and gently ask yourself what is this about for you. The more you lean into the emotions, the faster they can be released.

Imperfection is what makes it a masterpiece. It's what shows you that it was made by human hands and emotions.

Make the time to do something creative every day. You will be surprised at how much it feeds you. I found that working on the quilt for an hour of two after dinner was so satisfying in a way that surfing the Internet or watching TV couldn't compare.

What have you always wanted to try but didn't give yourself permission to because you didn't think you could do it? Allow yourself to be a beginner, that's where your creativity will blossom!

About the Author

LAURA HACKEL

Laura is a #1 bestselling author of the books "*I'm Having It*" and "*The Energy of Healing*." She is a vibrational energy healer and artist, wife, mother of three, writer, and bringer of light to this planet.

She can be found spending her days between her ceramics studio and her healing studio where she delights in helping people make a deeper connection to their soul and the wisdom of their souls and to experience the deep inner wisdom and beauty that exists in the layers, textures and patterns within.

Laura works her magic to help you raise your vibration and live the life you want by using her background as a corporate executive, her Shaman and energy healing training, her intuition and zest for life in general.

One of her favorite ways to clear out stuck energy and

bring in high vibrational energy is by playing the crystal bowls for groups and events. Each Bowl is made of quartz crystal and you have lay down and relax as she coaxes beautiful sounds from them that vibrate at the exact frequency you need to first release what it blocking you and then bring in the energy of what you desire. To hear the crystal bowls in action, visit her website at artfulhealings.com.

Laura also makes amazing vibrational Healing Vessels. Each Healing Vessel is formed with her own hands, to facilitate vibrational shifting in both your home and life. There are many shapes and sizes to choose from; each is one of a kind, lovingly handcrafted and sure to shift the energy of any space. Each Healing Vessel is infused with Healing Energy. To select the perfect healing vessel for you, visit artfulhealings.com. You can access her blog and event schedule at artfulhealings.com. Or you can connect on Facebook at Facebook.com/artful.healings.

Chapter 7

CREATIVITY: THE INFINITE SPACE OF INFINITE POSSIBILITY

By Dr. Lisa Cooney

Abuse is one of the biggest obstacles to creativity.

Well actually, truth be told, it's not the abuse itself. Often, by the time my clients come to see me, the abuse has ended. It may have been an isolated incident in their past or many experiences of abuse over decades.

Either way, when they come to me they describe a feeling of stuckness, like being trapped in an invisible cage. They describe this cage as being a destructive force that blocks them from fully creating their life.

So it's really the cage of abuse that is one of the biggest obstacles to creativity.

The Invisible Cage of Abuse

The cage of abuse perpetuates destruction, withdrawal, separation and isolation. When you are locked in the cage you are in a constant state of degrading and disempowering yourself.

If you've ever experienced abuse, you can get stuck in repeating patterns of the past abuse. Your health, relationships and money flows are all limited. Your generative and creative capacities to do what you love in the world become blocked.

It's like the needle gets stuck in the song track of, "I can't," "I don't know what to do" and "Something is wrong with me."

How can the fire of creativity burn when there is only stifling oppression?

How do you tap into the energy of creativity when you're locked in an invisible cage?

Destruction Prevails Over Creation

Instead of creating your life, you actually - unconsciously - choose the energy of destruction. In subtle yet pervasive ways you destroy everything you desire to create.

This may look like destroying or ending relationships, bankrupting yourself or indebting yourself financially, being destructive with your body and never realizing there is something else possible.

This may feel like you're paddling upstream, always confronting a struggle, obstacle or catastrophe.

Disharmony and conflict are familiar. Harmony and peace are foreign.

The invisible cage is rooted in the lie that something is wrong with you. It's based in a story that you are limited and that you lack something. These judgments that you make of yourself (and potentially others, too) are focused on destroying you and keeping you small. They are not geared to creating a life of radical aliveness.

I know this may sound insane. Why would anyone choose to destroy their life rather than create their life?

Yet ask yourself: have I been creating or destroying my life?

Have I been creating or destroying my relationship?

Have I been creating or destroying my relationship with myself?

Have I been creating or destroying my relationship with money?

Have I been creating or destroying my relationship with my body?

And be willing to be honest with yourself.

I Got Honest With Myself

I was very determined to use my own experience of abuse as the catalyst for the Beyond Abuse Revolution. Yet it required me getting honest with myself to see how I was actually destroying versus creating my life, relationships, career, finances, body, health and my whole being.

I, too, was once trapped in the invisible cage of abuse.

The first 2 decades of my life were filled with abuse: physical, sexual, emotional, mental, financial. It came from many places: family members, friends of family, the Church, the modeling agency, and healers.

I was told over and over all throughout my childhood that I was evil. I believed this lie. This lie became the cage that I lived in.

I never desired to let anyone close to me because I was afraid they, too, would see my evilness and run away screaming. How could I create anything other than destruction if I was evil and nobody would ever love me?

I learned the language of unkindness growing up. So that is what I used in relationship as an adult. I created conflict rather than communion, which resulted in divorce and desperation.

In my 20's I overrode my body's needs and engaged in destructive patterns: drugs, sex and overeating. I had money yet felt guilty that I had it and others didn't, so I paid for everyone else to try and buy their love.

All of these behaviors kept me trapped in the invisible cage of abuse, repeating the same abusive patterns that were familiar to me from my childhood. All I knew was to destroy myself and everything else in my life.

The Bridge Beyond The Cage

It wasn't till my 20's when a graduate school professor reached out to me and asked me if I was ok. This was a turning point. Up until that point in my life nobody had cared enough to ask.

My conversation with her was a turning point, and the bridge to a new chapter in my life. She helped me see there was another way of living beyond repeating the patterns of abuse. I became committed to finding the way out of the cage that kept me trapped in destruction rather than truly living my life.

I became a Doctor of Psychology. I studied dozens of healing modalities. I worked with therapists and healers. I simultaneously walked my own healing journey as I worked with clients, guiding them on their own healing journey beyond the invisible cage of abuse.

Over the past 2 decades I have worked with thousands of clients around the world. I am deeply humbled and grateful that the first 2 decades of my life, entrenched in so much abuse, became the catalyst for the Beyond Abuse Revolution: the community of people committed to joining together to kick abuse in the caboose.

I discovered the keys for unlocking the cage of abuse. And I am excited to share them with you here. Because beyond the cage, beyond the bridge, is a way of living that is rooted in the energy of possibility and creativity. This way of living is what I call, "Radically Alive."

Welcome To Radical Aliveness

Imagine waking up with a spring in your step, happy to be alive and ready to see what else is possible for the day. From start to finish, your day is full of choice based on your desires. From that desire, everything is possible and you are a generative and creative magnet. People love to be around you. You change the energy of everything around you just by being you.

Your relationships are based in communion and harmony. They are fun, easeful, joyful and mutual. Your body is healthy and vibrantly alive. You are energized. You have a special glow about you.

Your business is booming and the collaborators you have laugh and join with you in whatever you are creating. Each day is a new possibility of receiving money, support and possibilities.

Life is a joyous adventure. Laughter and lightness infuse your body. You are amazed to feel such an alliance with yourself.

People ask you what you did to change you and you respond with, "I chose me and happiness and created what I knew was possible."

Inspiring, isn't it?

Let me introduce you to the keys to unlock yourself from the cage of abuse, so you, too, can walk across the bridge and experience Radical Aliveness.

The 4 C's: Choose, Commit, Collaborate & Create

The 4 C's are keys that will unlock you from the lie and limitations you once bought into, and the destructive cycle that perpetuated your earlier abuse.

Ready? Let's go...

1. Choose You

What does it mean to "choose you"?

You know what it's like when you're in a relationship with someone and you do everything in support of them and not you?

That is an example of you NOT choosing you. When you do for others at the expense of yourself you are making them more important than you. This is what happens in abuse: your desires and needs become irrelevant.

Yet when you choose you, your needs and desires become important. You become a priority. You begin creating your life.

When you choose you - you can still be generous and be there for other people yet NOT at the expense of you. You include yourself in all your choices and relationships.

What might you create when you choose you?

2. Commit to You

When you commit to yourself, you commit to never giving in, never giving up, and never letting anyone or anything stop you. It's you committing to you to choose you every moment, every day.

In other words: you don't quit. Ever.

My tenacity to overcome the first 2 decades of my life and all the abuse I experienced came from this place of committing to me. Once I realized that I was living in a cage of abuse and that there was something I could choose beyond the cage, I vowed to never quit till I was out of the cage and on the other side of the bridge from it.

I also vowed to empower as many others as possible to unlock themselves from the cage of abuse by choosing themselves and committing to their own lives as well.

When you commit to yourself, you commit to being all of you in all of your relationships. You don't separate from yourself to try to please or accommodate others. As you commit to you, you're more available to commit to others in harmonious, mutually satisfying ways.

What might you create when you commit to you?

3. Collaborate with the Universe

Like I shared earlier, when you're inside the cage of abuse you may feel like you're paddling upstream and always confronting a struggle, obstacle or catastrophe.

You may feel like the world is out to get you.

I believed that for a long time, too. I thought everyone

was against me. I thought I had to do everything myself.

Yet I'm here to tell you: that is all a lie.

The Universe is actually conspiring to bless you. The Universe is actually rooting for your greatest joy and success.

When you collaborate with the Universe, you open yourself to receiving the contribution and support of all the different people and possibilities that DESIRE to give to you. You can use the questions I share in this chapter to open up to another kind of conversation with the Universe.

When you are willing to ask, and receive, you will discover that there is so much more available to you in creating your life.

What might you create when you collaborate with the Universe?

4. Create Your Life

What is fun for you? What lights you up?

How might your life be different if you created your life for you?

What would you choose for you when you're not focused on making other people your biggest priority?

When you keep tapping into what you desire and allow that to be your biggest priority, you will create an inspiring and expansive life for yourself. You will be the creator, rather than the destroyer of your life.

And truly, how does it get any better than that?

The Energy of Creativity

Using the 4 C's gets you out of the cage and across the bridge into radical aliveness, one step at a time, one choice at a time.

So rather than destroying your life, you are creating your life.

You must first choose to question the cage, and to see that it is made up of lies and limitations that are not true for you. You must be willing to let go of the old patterns of "I can't," "I don't know what to do," and "Something is wrong with me."

As you question the cage and ask what else is possible, you begin walking out of the cage and across the bridge to another possibility. The desire for something beyond the cage of abuse is the fuel that will carry you forward.

What is asking to be created now?

Choose it!

Viva La Revolution!

About The Author

DR. LISA COONEY

Dr. Lisa Cooney is a leading authority on thriving after childhood sexual abuse. As a licensed Marriage and Family Therapist, certified Access Consciousness Facilitator, Master Theta Healer and author of the upcoming book, "Kick Abuse in the Caboose: The Bridge to Radical Aliveness," she has supported thousands of people over the past 20 years move beyond their abuse to create infinite possibilities for themselves.

Lisa experienced sexual, physical and emotional abuse herself from the time she was a baby into her early 20s. Having found the key to unlock herself from the cage of abuse, Lisa has now committed her life to revolutionizing the approach to trauma. She is known for using pragmatic tools to create quantum change. Visit her site to find out more about her Beyond Abuse Revolution, LLC and to access her Free Gifts: www.DrLisaCooney.com.

Chapter 8

LUSCIOUS LEADERSHIP

By Danna Lewis

What if committing to your life is the creation point for everything you desire?

I'm sitting in my boyfriend's living room strumming the two chords I know on one of his guitars. I'm practicing the two chords he taught me individually and am not yet able to flow between them with any sense of ease or grace. I stop one note, look at the image on the 'learn to play guitar' app on my iPhone he sweetly sent me for tutoring and awkwardly place my fingers on the other note and start strumming. Then I count, I count and I strum. And I'm pretty darn happy that it's all working to whatever extent it's working and there's a pretty sound being produced. I let go of everywhere it's suppose to be right, good and perfect to my implanted standard and structure and let myself free-fall into the magnanimous interaction of abundance that the Universe provides. What if in this earthy, acoustical space I can orchestrate an entire Universe of change and possibility? What if the nurturing, healing, joyful, expansive energy of guitar playing can contribute to me and my body, my life and my living in a way that is so not linear or grounded in form, structure and significance? What if the simple act of asking my boyfriend to teach me guitar, his nurturing kindness in teaching, my raw 'I'm afraid to not look good at something in front of him' and learn something I do not know opens me up to a level of receiving that did not exist before he placed my hands on the strings? Beyond the structure and between the molecules there is an energy of creativity.

I'm standing in my closet asking my body what it would like to wear. "Body, what would you like to wear today?" "No, naked is not one of the options right now especially if we plan to leave the house today." "Nothing, reallll-lyyyy, all these clothes and there is nothing you would choose today?" "Ummm, okay, if you could have any clothes you desired, what would that be?" And my body shows me images of dresses for date night; dresses for strolling around town; outfits for meeting with clients; simple, chic shirts with a feminine flair; and jackets, we love jackets! "Seriously body, all of that? We're building a business here, where do you think all of that can come from? Where is the money coming from and when would we even have the time to go to all the stores to get such a variety of new clothes?"

A month or so later I'm asking another question, "If it wasn't about money, would I drive or fly to Encinitas for my visit with Jessie?" Drive was the whisper of awareness. On my third day in Encinitas, we are downstairs in Jessie's laundry room and she starts pulling out clothes for me. Beautiful, chic, fun, edgy, feminine, we literally share the same head because I so would have chosen these things for myself clothes. One after the other she's handing me dresses, skirts, shirts, jackets and they all

The Energy of Creativity

fit like they were made for my body which is interesting since Jessie is smaller than me. Three bags later we are both giggling like schoolgirls because of the gift of giving and receiving and sheer fun of an afternoon fashion show in the garage.

Control freak minds pops in- "how are we getting all this home?" Brilliant body replies, "remember the whole fly or drive thing?" It all goes in the car and it never would have gotten home if I had flown down and not listened to the whispers of awareness. And then I hear it…my body, my brilliant, beautiful, sassy body says, "Hey, remember when you were all form, structure and significance about this new wardrobe I desired?" I laugh out loud. Beyond the structure and between the molecules there is an energy of creativity.

I'm chatting with a girlfriend about a 'Being You, Changing the World' class in Ft. Lauderdale, Florida last year and she says, "See you there." I can feel the smirk on her face and wedgy in my Universe. No, no, no Lauren, I'm not going 3,000 miles across the country for a class, just no; it's not for me. And yet, in that same instance I do my reach out into all the corners of my awareness across all time and space and perceive through the Universe the magnitude of change I can create by actually being at this class.

My father, whom I haven't seen in about 10 years lives in this city, I'll be in a class with my 'big brother of consciousness,' so to speak, Dr. Dain Heer and there it is - the very juicy invitation to change in the biggest way possible 45 years of 'daddy crap'. Oh, but I say no way, no how I am going to a class on the other side of the country. A month later I did go to a class in Los Angeles (and drove down from San Francisco). I meet a guy in that class; hook up, so to speak, start dating and a few weeks later I'm on a plane to visit him and his kids in South Carolina. The trip gets extended, I'm asked to make invitation phone calls for the class that I had previously refused to go to that is now a few states away instead of across the country. And there it is, a road trip from South Carolina to Ft. Lauderdale with my friend and his kids to attend the class that is now free because I've spent about 20 hours on the phone doing work for the host team. And what was looked at, cleared and changed in that class has catapulted my entire life, living and love. With that quiet demand for consciousness, for change and for creation, I went beyond the structure and between the molecules to the energy of creativity.

I'm in my head bouncing back and forth trying to figure something out, another something, another millionth bounce of the ball in my head and my body, my brilliant, sweet, potent body says, "re-arrange the furniture" or "go swimming" or "go running' or "bounce on the mini trampoline" please. Please stop hurting my head trying to figure everything out. So I start re-arranging the furniture and half-way through I realize this is exactly what will work to have the apartment look and feel more like an office for clients and to accommodate about 10 people for a class! Another time I went swimming, and lap after lap of thoughts dissipating their electromagnetic charge in the saline pool water, an entire class appears in my head, and another time an entire website I have yet to build. Or I go running and as I'm pounding out my crazy-ass limiting points of view onto the pavement the realization and acknowledgment that all the clutter and crap that was there before was actually a creation too.

What would occur if I did a 180 and pulled all of my energy out of the contraction I bought into and created and flowed it into the forward, generative space of possibility? Beyond all the structure of what each of those activities is supposed to be and between the molecules there is an energy of creativity.

I'm nursing a heartbreak, complete utter failure I dramatize in my head while the rest of me is all "what's right about this I'm getting?" And while I'm crying, getting my Bars® run (Access Consciousness Bars®) and being with the intensity of pain and vulnerability that comes with a breakup, I do four things that change the course of my life… I ask a lot of questions, I acknowledge that no matter how or what I'm judging this event as I created it, my body and I demand the change for what we actually desire and require…then we ask the Universe for it. We don't just ask with words, we perceive the energy of "Delicious We." We create a sphere of that energy and reach out millions of miles in all directions and pull energy through the entire Universe to contribute to this thing that we know is so possible and have not yet actualized. Then we let little trickles of that yum go back out into the Universe like an energetic text message so that the quantum entanglements can come together to create this energy into a tangible life force. Several months later and a million moments after that preciously potent ask, a single swipe to the right on a dating app actualized into a delicious we that shook the suspension of disbelief out of me to a core of 'I so know I am a creator of magnitude and the Universe has my back!' What else is possible beyond the structure of this reality and between the molecules where the blissful buzz of the energy of creativity lives?

What do you actually desire in your life, living and love? What if the lack and avoidance of allowing yourself to know that bastardizes the blissful buzz of creative energy into the destroying living of creative energy? What could change if you acknowledged that underneath all of it, all the joy and sadness, all the rightness and wrongness, all the good and bad the one common theme is you? What if that's okay? What if that's the true beauty of creation? What if that raw intimacy with yourself nurtures you into a different possibility?

What do you actually require to create and actualize the life, living and love you desire? What if knowing your priorities and knowing what you desire isn't enough? What if the knowing is the creation point? When my boyfriend and I say we love each other, often we'll stop and chat about the loving actions that are required to actually create 'the yum' of our relationship that we've identified as a priority in our lives. We look at what it can contribute to each of us and allow ourselves to be aware of what it gifts the world. We use it as a creation point for something greater. What if knowing your priorities is the creation point of actualizing this thing called life exponentialized into your juiciest reality? What if what's truly required is to be the Luscious Leader of you? And what if committing to be the Luscious Leader of you empowers you beyond the structure of this reality and between the molecules to the ease, joy and gratitude of the energy of creativity… where anything is possible and everything is yours?

About The Author

Danna Lewis

Danna Lewis, Global Change Facilitator, #1 bestselling author and Conscious Leadership Coach, has over 20 years of business experience and trainings, certifications and education in consciousness and empowerment coaching. She works with clients and business through customized sessions and classes designed to clear limitations while providing pragmatic tools and strategy that will create the space for something greater to exist. This is where the rubber meets the road in the creative edge for exceeding desired results.

 Her clients appreciate the kindness, empowerment and levity she brings to the work. She thrives on what is possible to create together with clients and class participants. Her Luscious Leadership platform contributes to that "… richly fulfilling and enjoyable space of guiding, influencing and directing yourself with empowered effectiveness to create a life, living and love that work deliciously well for you."

She is an Access Consciousness@ and Joy of Business® Certified Facilitator. Highlights from her corporate experience include building high performance work teams of happy, empowered employees on Wall Street, managing 400 million dollar bank accounts for the world's largest banking institution, creating revenue streams in a zero-sum revenue operations department, and directing brand management and social media architecture for a luxury exercise franchise tripling in size during her tenure.

Danna knows it is possible to thrive in all the spaces of our lives and that by eliminating the artificial walls of limitation, more contribution and receiving can exist. That levity and gratitude and kindness can be incredibly potent forces of change. That choice and question can always provide the possibilities to out-create anything. Danna currently lives with her boyfriend, Robert, (aka as #sexychef) in their San Francisco home weekdays and Monterey, CA home on the weekends with his six year-old son.

Chapter 9

CREATIVITY IS MAGIC

By Tara Thelen

What's this thing that happens when you're being creative?

For me, it's a kind of magic.

There is something that happens when I'm painting, for example, that is outside of technique or "using the right side of my brain." It doesn't happen all the time, only sometimes actually, this thing that happens—where creativity takes on a whole different *something*.

Like I said, it's a kind of magic. It just slices through what I am doing, what I am painting. My hand is holding the brush, putting it to canvas, and my brain is telling me what I need to do. These things get pushed aside, or become secondary I should say, and what happens is amazing. It's a form of channeling.

Several years ago, I was creating a portrait of John Lennon and I had a photo to go by, paints all set up, space to paint, etc., and then that something amazing happened: the magic! I was about 15 minutes into the painting and I went into some kind of trance or began to channel or something and I literally lost myself in the process of creating. The technique and method and conscious planning melted away and I went into a different state of mind, a perfect CREATIVE state of mind, without judgment, without bias, without the interference of rational thinking. What came about was a pure connection with my subject and the energy and creative energy that mingled. I remember thinking, when I finished, "who did that" and "how did that happen"? I had literally invested blood (I had cut my finger slightly when I was wiping paint from my palette knife), sweat (lots of it) and tears (when I looked at the final portrait and was overwhelmed by the energy of it). What's interesting to note is that I don't think I was the only one that felt a certain energy in that portrait, because it ultimately ended up (completely unexpectedly and "coincidentally") being used for the cover of a John Lennon book (that was given to Yoko Ono) years later. Where does this creativity come from? I wonder about this a lot because I don't feel it has to do directly with want, talent, drive or interest or anything of those outside forces, but comes instead from an intrinsic force, a dynamic energy that we all have within us and can spur us on at any time. It probably helps to have materials to work with to get our creativity out into something tangible. Knowledge of specific techniques also can help in how we go about releasing our creative energies. Or, maybe it just helps to have an open mind and be open to being creative and applying our creativity to any aspect of our lives.

So, there's this creativity that exists on all levels and in all different forms. How would I describe it? I would describe creativity as a rainbow of colors, a full prism of this really great, uplifting energy that brightens up the steel-gray aspects of our existence.

Creativity knows no bounds. Everything is possible - for each of us. Because it's our own creativity, unique to us, and this means it's always "right," on any level, in any form, through any medium. All we need to do is give ourselves over to it, and trust in it, and feel it and let it lift us and make us better.

It's probably best described as the process of just totally losing yourself…

Which is most likely where you find yourself!

About the Author

TARA THELEN

Tara Thelen is an American artist living near Amsterdam. Her artwork has been exhibited in galleries throughout the US, Europe, and the Pacific. The inspiration for her work is emotion, in all its various forms.

As an artist, Tara's drive is to create art that elicits strong, positive emotions – art that leaves an impression and truly touches those who view it.

Tara creates book cover designs and illustrations, and works on various commercial projects with Deborah Perdue of Illumination Graphics (who is also a contributing author in this book) and teaches art lessons to children and teens at Museum Kranenburgh in the beautiful village of Bergen, near the North Sea, where she lives with her husband Paul and their two teenage boys.

www.Tara-artwork.com

Chapter 10

CO-CREATING WITH YOUR GUIDES AND ANGELS

By Andy Pentecost

Do you know what you would like to create in your life however you are not sure how to get there? Or do you have a feeling that you were put on this earth to share your knowledge, tools or wisdom although you are not yet aware of what that is?

I have had a feeling for years that I would write a book, have it published and it would contribute to the lives of many people. I wasn't sure what it was about or how I would make it happen.

I was introduced to Access Consciousness about 7 or 8 years ago and completed many of the available courses. I was hungry for change and these tools really worked for me. One very important tool taught in Access is to ask questions. A question opens up your choices or opportunities and a statement closes them down. A statement can restrict and constrain you and your options. For example: If you are feeling tired and you say "I'm tired." You have just told the Universe and your body that you are tired. So what shows up from here? More tiredness, heaviness, and fatigue. What if you asked, "what would it take to have more energy here or more energy now"? Does that have your body feel lighter and more inspired?

Or you might wish to ask another Access question, "Is this mine, or who does this belong to" If you relax, your shoulders drop, you take a deep breath or have the awareness that it's not yours then say "I let this go." You can use this anytime you are experiencing things that you don't normally feel, think, say or if you have any pain in your body. Did you know that you can't let something go, that's not yours unless you are aware or acknowledge that it's not yours in the first place? Once you have acknowledged it you can let it go.

Are you also aware that 98% of your thoughts, feelings and emotions are not even yours? We are such empathic beings that we pick up on or take on other peoples, thoughts, feelings and emotions and store them as though they are our own. "Cute but not smart" as Dr Dain Heer says, Co-Creator of Access Consciousness.

What we are doing here is asking questions of our Guides and Angels, the Universe, Your Higher Self or Inner Knowing, or God. Whichever term resonates with you, use that going forward or what works for you. I will refer to it as Guides and Angels. Effectively what is happening is we are asking for help with the things that we don't know or the things that we do know that we would like to change or create faster. This is Co-Creating with your Guides and Angels. The biggest thing to remember in all of this is to be open minded about how it will show up. If you have a fixed point of view about how it will show up this interferes with the creative energy. For example: If you have a preconceived idea, it has to be like this, this,

The Energy of Creativity

this or this otherwise it won't be perfect. What if it could be better than your perfect? It's as if you are ordering from the Menu of the Universe, you know what it is you wish to order, you order it, and sit back and enjoy your surroundings, and let the restaurant take care of the rest, and your meal appears right! Would you ever follow a waitress into the kitchen and tell the chef how to do his job and prepare your meal? I don't think so, so don't do that with your Guides and Angels either, because if you do:

a) it might not turn out half as well as it could have

b) you may have slowed down the process or stopped it completely.

Allow it to unfold however it unfolds the wisdom of the Universe has a lot more experience than you or I do. What if what was to come out of your question or your order was far greater than you ever thought was possible, just by TRUSTING?

It's not about ordering and sitting back on your tooshie and doing absolutely nothing either. When you ask a question you create an energy or a feeling. When an opportunity arises that aligns with what you have been asking for, it will carry the same energy or feeling. It's all about following that energy. Normally when you follow the energy of what you have asked for it will feel light and be easy. It all falls into place. The key, is being willing to follow the energy.

For example: I was in a meditation group a few years ago and we were given the task of making a dream board as part of our homework. One of things on my dream board was a car. It was a Holden SS Commodore, V8, 6 speed manual, with black leather seats and black in colour. I had owned a red one within the past year. This time I wanted a black one, with a view to having it signwritten in the future. I knew what it smelt like, what it would feel like, what it would sound like and by creating the dream board I had asked my Guides and Angels for it. I had been quite specific.

I had the awareness to speak to a guy I had worked with, who knew someone at the Holden dealership in Hamilton. He spoke to a guy on Friday who rang me the following Monday. He said we have one in the yard right now, however it has red leather seats (getting a pre-loved manual car wasn't as accessible as an automatic, so I was like WOW that was fast). Although I didn't want red leather seats, he convinced me to go over and drive it anyway. It felt light so I went. I loved it as I knew I would. I still wasn't sold on the red leather seats though. He said "Ok so what if we take the black leather seats out of this car and put them in yours and change the door inserts for the black ones as well and put the tow bar from this one onto yours. Would you be interested? "OF COURSE!" And it all fell into place and was easy.

They traded my car, gave me a manual loan car to drive home in, more brownie points. I met the salesman halfway two days later to pick up my new car. If I hadn't followed the energy, and when he said it had red seats, I had said No, it would have stopped the whole process in its tracks and confused my Guides and Angels. Instead it all fell into place and I got my new car. It was that easy and that FAST. I had no idea what was going to happen, however I was ready to trust and follow the energy because it felt the same as what I had been asking for.

In the meantime we had had another meditation group where we shared our dream boards and I was able to say,

The Energy of Creativity

I was picking my new car up later that week. That's how fast it can happen when you are willing to follow the energy.

Sometimes when things happen that fast we can freak out and go "oh it can't happen that fast, there must be something wrong." Again we can stop it. If it feels right go with the flow and allow it.

Where have you been unwilling to follow the energy and your inner knowing, that if you were willing to follow it would create way more change and opportunities in your life than you ever thought was possible? Everything that doesn't allow that unlock it, unblock it and let it go.

Another example: During our stay in Australia in April this year, we were scheduled to pick up a rental car at 3pm, to go to the Blue Mountains for a few days. We had arrived in Gosford early, so my partner Gary suggested we swing by the rental place and fill out the paperwork because sometimes it can take awhile and if it was going to cost more to take it early, then we would come back after doing some shopping and collect the car at the scheduled time. Sure that would be great.

Just before we got there I had the awareness to ask, "I wonder what it would take to get an upgrade," Gary said, "that would be nice."

We walked in and talked to the lady and after a little discussion she told us we would be getting a Toyota Corolla instead of a Hyundai I20, which we had booked. Cool but is that actually an upgrade, I wasn't sure. It was also going to cost us another ¼ day for taking it early, so we said we would come back. She said we couldn't do the paperwork until we were ready to collect it as it is all hooked up to the computer times etc and it would only take five minutes. Ok what else is possible?

So off we went to do a bit of shopping and catch up with Gary's daughter. At just after 3pm we arrived back. We filled out the paperwork and another lady went outside and pulled a car up outside the front door. It was a Nissan Altima which is about the same size as the Toyota Camry. I nudged Gary and said "there is our upgrade." He said, "I don't think so."

Then the lady behind the desk gave us the keys and went through the blemishes on the car on a piece of paper and said "it's the one out the front, we have given you a bit of an upgrade." We thanked her very much and sent up a big thank you to our guides and angels. We were both so grateful. It had way more leg room and space. We easily fitted our luggage in. It was smooth on the road and made our holiday so much nicer. How does it get any better than that?

When we were due to fly back to New Zealand, I said "I wonder what it would take to get an upgrade?" Gary agreed. I asked at the desk as we checked in and they said they didn't just upgrade people anymore however we should ask at the boarding gate because if they knew we were interested then it could be possible.

We got to the gate and I thought, no if we are supposed to be upgraded it will happen. It turned out we were on a smaller plane and there were only 3 seats on each side and no business class. (interesting!) We sat in our seats and had paid for the works which included food and movies. After a little while we both realised our video screens weren't working and there were a few others around us having the same difficulty. We talked to one of the flight attendants and he said he would reset them. If

The Energy of Creativity

there was still a problem they would sort it out in the air.

It worked while they were running through the safety video and then it stopped. At least we knew what to do in case of an emergency right! Once in the air, the flight attendant came back and said don't worry we will move you since you have paid for movies and your meals will be redirected. So we were moved, asked which meals we would like and we received our meals first. We were offered a drink each and then within 10 to 15 minutes another flight attendant checked on us and refilled our drinks.

We may not have been upgraded to business class but we did get special treatment. How does it get any better than that? Remember it doesn't always look like you think it will.

What invitation could you be to have miracles and magic show up in your life?

When you ask questions and are willing to follow the energy of that, things start to open up and life flows. Life is so much easier when you are in the flow instead of going against the current. Here are some generative questions that may be helpful to get you back in the flow and follow your Genius/Talents and Abilities.

Where in my life am I going against the flow, that if I were to go with the flow would create and generate everything I have been asking for with ease?

What is stuck in my life that if it was unstuck would give me far greater awareness of who I truly am?

What awareness am I missing that if it was present would give me far greater freedom and knowing?

What would have to shift and change within me for me to embrace my true Talents and Abilities?

What am I afraid of, that if I was to become aware of it and release it, would give me so much more freedom and ease in all areas of my life?

What if what is overwhelming me, is really an illusion, something I have bought into or someone else's, how much more could I create and generate in my life? And/or my business?

What else is possible here that I have not been aware of? What question could I ask here that would make a difference?

Are you ready to follow the energy and your Genius/Talents and Abilities to create whatever it is that you have always known you were put on this earth to do? Everything that doesn't allow that unlock it, unblock it and let it go.

My intention with this chapter is to encourage you and give you tools that enable you to step into who you really BE. Your true Genius/Talents and Abilities are required in the world and they **do** make a difference. Be the YOU, YOU were born to BE!

About the Author

ANDY PENTECOST

Andy Pentecost is a Transformational Life Coach, Intuitive, Healer of Magnitude, Animal Communicator and Psychic.

Andy (Andrea) was born in a small town called Hawera, one hour away from New Plymouth in New Zealand. Her family shifted to Oparau just outside of Kawhia on the west coast of the North Island when she was about 3 and a half.

They moved to Tirau, which is between Cambridge and Rotorua, two weeks before she turned 5. She grew up in a dry stock farming community and could ride horses from the time she could walk. Her schooling was in Tirau, Putaruru and Matamata, which are all within 30 minutes of each other. She never ventured far from where she grew up and lived in Rotorua for almost 20 years.

Andy met Gary four years ago and this is the most connected she has ever felt to anyone. "He lights up my life, and supports me no matter what and we love each other without judgment, we are both on the same wavelength and wish to make a difference in the world." They moved themselves, her son and their businesses to Tauranga eighteen months ago and they both love the lightness of area. The energy and the sea is a big draw card for Andy as it helps her stay connected and clear.

She has been working within the Natural Health and Healing field for the past 18 years. She was led into Therapeutic Massage as her son Sidney was born with a clubfoot. Seeing the difference it made for him, (walking at one year of age and doing everything normally without surgery) she embarked on her training to be a Massage Therapist to enable her to help as many people as she could. Andy has two boys, Sidney is 19 and Bailey is 15. She was prescribed hormone tablets to get pregnant with her Sidney. With both children she was diagnosed with postnatal depression (PND) and after having Bailey it was more severe than after Sidney.

She went through orthodox medical treatments, this meant taking antidepressants, which had balanced things enough so that she could explore alternative therapies and on a friend's recommendation, she started having her chakras balanced. At this time she was taking four antidepressants per day and within nine months of starting to have her chakras balanced regularly which included working through some things she had emotionally suppressed during her life she was able to stop all medications.

In total she lived with postnatal depression for around 7 years. Once well, she learnt how to balance Chakras and she introduced this into her own clinical work, so that she could facilitate even more change for people. She is also a trained Reiki Master Teacher.

Andy came across Access Consciousness® around seven years ago and through her own experience, knows how much it has changed her life, those of her clients and the people around her. This is when she introduced Intuitive Life Coaching into her clinical practise.

After working with many clients over the past 18 years, Andy's experience is that it is important to balance the Mental, Emotional, Physical and Spiritual aspects of our bodies and beings. This creates peace and harmony within your lives.

Over the years Andy has diversified the modalities she uses and works very intuitively with each person to achieve the desired result of each client. She has seen how the physical bodies hold emotions and has developed techniques whereby she talks to the body and soul to give it permission to release whatever it is holding from whatever lifetime it was locked in. This can be done in person, or via phone/ Skype.

Earlier this year Andy realized it was time to stop talking about finishing her book and take action to do it. She asked her Guides and Angels, "What's it going to take to get my book published? What is it that I am supposed to be doing?" What is it going to take to make a Global Difference and Fast?

Originally she felt the book would be published and linked to Access Consciousness although she didn't know what that would look like. She explored different avenues and had chosen at that point to self publish through create space, downloading a template and transferring her book into it.

Andy had come to a point in her life when she knew that to make the global impact that she had been put on this planet to do, would require major change.

She watched a google hangout for a book launch with Erica Glessing, Rebecca Hulse and Cory Michelle. The book was called "The Energy of Receiving." The book resonated with what she had been asking for and she ordered it. The book and tools were amazing and created the shift she had been asking for. Now was the time! She was drawn to email Erica at Happy Publishing.

They had a skype conversation, and Andy found that she was easy to talk to and totally understood her. In the space of 15 minutes, she had honed in on where the book had been stopped and how it felt. Erica ran a clearing and everything lightened up and Andy's heart opened like it never had before. Erica has an amazing gift. (Thank you Erica, for gifting the book back its life). Erica felt into the energy of the book which is amazing and suggested asking questions. Who would you like to have publish you? What would you like it to look like? Who would you like to contribute to?

Andy sat with the book and had the awareness of what the book required and emailed Erica back. The book has now been birthed. "Angel Guidance to Connection, Strength and Magic" and is available on Amazon http://www.amazon.com/Angel-Guidance-Connection-Strength-Magic/dp/0989633284, or if you are in New Zealand or Australia it is available on her website below.

If you have a book inside you and have been waiting' is NOW the right time? If so, I would highly recommend Erica. She is an amazing publisher/editor to work with. She is highly intuitive and she will support you along with your book throughout the entire process.

To connect with Andy or to know more about how she works, her website is www.andypentecost.com, https://www.facebook.com/andypentecosttransformationspecialist, or info@andypentecost.com.

Chapter 11

CREATIVITY IS EVERYWHERE

By Deborah Perdue

Art makes life bearable. It isn't a luxury. Like our capacity for understanding, and our experience of love, it is a vitally important part of life.
~ Gillian Pederson Krag

One thing I absolutely know and believe is that the entire universe is resplendently creative; nature herself is constantly in flux and abundantly creative, with her own divine timing, and ebbs and flows of growth and shedding.

The whole universe is alive and creating! And always has been, from the moment of the Big Bang, or whatever started the whole thing, to right now – ancient stars exploding, new worlds emerging. And on this precious earth, volcanoes erupt changing the land. Rivers flow and change the landscape each season. Spring appears, and out come the tulips and daffodils and lilacs abloom, going into summer with its big deep orange oriental poppies, multi colored dahlias, sunflowers and the fragrances of lavender and rosemary bursting forth. The trees dress up in their regalia after the dormancy and barrenness of winter. Nature puts on an extravaganza of an art show at every moment. Every single day clouds shape-shift in the sky. Dramatic sunsets and dawns show off their streaks of tangerine and peach and deep pinks. All of this is so very creative and wondrously beautiful. And what about the spirals of galaxies? And what about the spiral make-up of sunflower heads, pinecones and nautilus shells? How mysterious and creative is that, that so much of nature and even our bodies follow a mathematical Fibonacci progression? WOW!

I believe that the Divine permeates everything and everyone. So we witness the divine creating and expressing in colorful, majestic ways constantly in Mother Nature.

And just like Nature, I believe that every single one of us IS creative. Every single one of us, without exception, have creative gifts and talents to share. It is part of our innate essence as human beings to create.

I teach spiritual classes and I have noticed when we talk about creativity, some people clam up immediately, feeling that if they don't draw or paint or write or play music, they are not creative. Yes, the musicians and poets and artists are obviously creative. What about the Mom or Dad who instinctively knows how to play with their children? What about a person who can motivate, inspire and energize others in the workplace? What about a bookkeeper or CPA who plays with number crunching and finds mathematics joyful? I claim that creativity comes in a myriad of forms, and whenever we feel a sense of losing track of time when we are immersed in our particular path, then that is the clue that we ARE creative!

And it is so natural to be in the creative flow. It is less natural to halt the flow of creativity. I am convinced that

The Energy of Creativity

we are spiritual beings having a human experience, as it is so often stated these days. And as I already pointed out, Spirit is ALWAYS creative.

All that being said, (and I firmly believe every word), I must admit that I've been experiencing writer's block around this subject matter. All of my life I have been a creative person, and all of my life I have fought with an inner critic who keeps warning me that I am not a real artist – that I am not really creative. Others who are close to me – like my sisters, husband, friends and clients – have always believed in my talents and abilities much more than I have.

If I look back on my life, from the time I was a little girl, I wrote in diaries and journals. It was natural and even thrilling to me, to share my thoughts on paper. I remember as a young student, probably 2nd grade, a peak moment for me was when a teacher took us out to look at trees and flowers one Spring, and I can remember being absolutely enchanted, and having so much fun pressing leaves and flowers afterwards. At 9 or 10, I recall sitting in a blooming bright-yellow acacia tree near our house, day after day after school, communing with the splendor, magic and beauty of those trees and their feather-light blossoms. During my childhood, I also wrote poems and made little books of them that my mother adored. And I could draw! My sisters were in awe of me.

As a teen, I took Advanced Placement English classes in high school because I excelled in expressing myself on paper. I remember trying my hand at ceramics, and adoring a jewelry-making class. In college, it was a natural progression to take creative writing classes, and also photography classes – in fact, I double-majored in English and Art because I couldn't decide between them. I got absolutely lost in creativity in the darkroom, with dodging, burning and perfecting my black and white photography.

All of my adult life, I have been a graphic designer, now focusing on book design. This is a highly creative job that satisfies the artist in me. I have published several books, and I write blogs and articles. I am an avid journal keeper. I have published several books, the *Grace of Gratitude Journal*, *Grace of Gratitude Journal Vol. 2* and *Grace of Gratitude Reflections*. I also wrote a chapter for the book *The Energy of Expansion*. I write blogs and articles that are published in local newspapers and online. I send out Daily Gratitude Affirmations to my email list. I continue with my daily Gratitude journaling and also journaling feelings and thoughts in a second journal.

About 15 years ago, I fell in love with creating pastel drawings, and took classes, so immersed in the joy of rubbing and blending colors on paper. I evolved to color digital photography because color is so important to my soul. When I moved to Oregon, I found that it is the home of exquisite natural beauty of forest after forest, mountains and rivers, and I have taken literally thousands and thousands of photos because I have been so inspired. This is a sideline passion for me. Last year, an online magazine featured my photography on their site, and that was a thrill! I am especially fascinated with the play of reflections in water, and have been known to race outside to capture a particularly amazing sunset before it fades away.

I know, also, that I am creative with home decorating, intuitively feeling the Feng Shui of balance and harmony. I dress artistically in gorgeous rich colors and flowing shawls and long skirts.

The Energy of Creativity

My inner critic also likes to tell me that what I do creatively is not enough; that compares me to other incredible artists like my soul sister Tara Thelen and lets me know I do not measure up. And even though I know that comparison is not fruitful, I sometimes let self-doubts enter my consciousness when I am vulnerable to that critic within.

So, instead of listening to the critic who tries to bring me down, I choose to listen to all I have said in this chapter! To know that I DO measure up. I am a flowing, creative vessel of the Divine, and every single day I am creating! My whole life, in fact, is a magnificent creation, despite any inner opinion to the contrary! And so is your life.

1. If you are like me and sometimes doubt your creativity, I invite you to reflect on and answer these questions:

2. When do I lose track of time? What am I doing when that happens?

3. Do others see me as creative? Can I let their opinions help me to realize that I am?

4. What unconventional ways am I creative?

5. Am I so good at something that it is like second nature to me?

Let your own critical voices pipe down, and appreciate your own natural abilities and talents, and find the creativity within you, and let it shine!

"With the word "Creative" we stand under a mystery. And from time to time that mystery, as if it were a sun, sends down upon one head or another,

a sudden shaft of light – by grace, one feels, rather than deserving, for it always is something given, free, unsought, unexpected."
  ~ Pamela Travers, *Creators on Creating*

About the Author

DEBORAH PERDUE

Deborah Perdue is a writer, an accomplished book designer, and an avid nature photographer. Ms. Perdue is the author of two *Grace of Gratitude Journals*, *Grace of Gratitude Reflections*, and has also authored a chapter in the book *Energy of Expansion*. She writes on the topics of spirituality, gratitude, and bringing more peace and joy into our lives, in her own blog, as well as in local newspaper articles and ezines. She sends out Daily Gratitude Affirmations through the Grace of Gratitude website.

Chapter 12

ADVENTURES OF CREATING

By Betsy McLoughlin

What is creation? What have you defined creation as? What does it look like, smell like, feel like? Have you decided you aren't creative?

Have you noticed when you are playing and creating time melts away? Whatever creating and generating is for you. It could be cooking a yummy meal, drawing or doodling, coloring, writing, creating a beautiful garden of flowers or vegetables. It could be renovating a home or tuning up your car. How about playing music or cleaning your home? Organizing your closet, dancing around the living room are more examples of creating. I bet most people don't think about cleaning their home, doing laundry or writing a proposal for the office as creating. This is definitely a different way to think about creations! If you were joyfully cleaning out the closet, what contribution would that be to shifting the energy from obligation to joy?

We are creating all the time. Creating crap, sadness or depression. We also create joy, expansion and happiness.

The Adventures of Creativity — Betsy McLoughlin

I lived a lot of my life creating crap, depression, illness, trauma and drama and am choosing different now! I'm choosing joy, expansion, possibilities, happiness and more. What can I contribute to actualizing creations now in this space?

I used to own a craft store and would lose all track of time creating art in many different forms. I would forget to drink or eat. I would sit down for a few minutes and the next thing I know, 2 or more hours elapsed like it was 10 minutes. I enjoy teaching people how to design cards, jewelry and altered books. I taught many people how to look at themselves as artists. Many had never thought of themselves in this light before. To see them appreciate and enjoy their creations was so amazing and rewarding.

I used to create something and critiqued it as lacking or ugly and would throw it out. One day, my son went to the trash and gave it back to me and told me "Mommy, this is pretty, don't throw it out." Looking at the creation the next day from a different perspective showed me how I could tweak something or add some elements and have it morph into something different. And it became beautiful in my eyes. How many places in our lives have we decided something was ugly or awful without asking questions? What if that bland dish you created just needed a little salt or other seasonings? Would you be willing to add ingredients and change things around instead of throwing the dish out?

What choices do you have now that you didn't have a minute ago? If you are energy in the future, the past and now – what would it take to use that to your advantage?

Are you willing to be the catalyst to whatever is asking to be born? When the invitation caresses you on the cheek

The Energy of Creativity

and whispers in your ear, do you listen? What could that look like? It could be a book, a song, or a new recipe. Are you willing to receive the creation as it expresses itself? Are you listening to the dance asking to be composed? What contribution can we be to the energy, space and consciousness for a different possibility? What would be joyful for us to contribute to?

Have you thought about creating your day to be an adventure? What can you do that would create something different from yesterday? Unlimited adventures are possible to create. Are you willing to create a grand adventure no matter what you are doing?

Would you be willing to eliminate everywhere you decided creating has to be hard and ask questions instead? When you ask questions, you open up the door for many different opportunities. What would it take for this to be ease and joyful playtime?

I was talking to a friend on the phone about some ideas I had. I stated that I would love to be on telesummits. I asked, "I wonder how that is possible?" I stayed in the space of wouldn't it be awesome and then I forgot about it. I had no conclusion or judgment if or when it would even show up.

A few days later, I opened my email to find an invitation from a Facebook friend whom I've never met in person. She told me she thought I was awesome and asked if I would like to participate in a telesummit she was creating! What? You know who I am? Oh wow! Yes please, I would be honored to participate.

Another idea I had was how fun it would be to be a published author. I began writing in a journal and have lots of material there for a book. The book does not desire to be born yet. I ask this book to let me know when it desires more attention. In the meantime, I have been asked to collaborate in several books and am having a blast! Those books all asked for my energy and it was a yes to play with them! My first book collaboration became a best seller! Oh my gosh, how lucky am I?

I would like to give you an example of a conclusion I went to. A friend invited me to collaborate in a book that had a lot of yummy energy. I asked her what the book was about and almost instantly I decided I had nothing to contribute to this book. I forgot to ask the book if it desired my contribution. I forgot to ask myself if it would be light and juicy in my world. I slammed the door shut on possibilities by concluding and not asking any questions. Oopsie - how cute! This was a good reminder to me to always ask questions!

Can you create adventures today? What if you have an interaction with the bank teller and change their day with a smile and an acknowledgment they are doing a great job? I love playing and interacting with people I come in contact with. Most of the time, the people enjoy talking and smiling. Sometimes the people don't choose to play or smile and that's ok – it's their choice.

Here are some questions to play with:

- What would joy bring into my life?
- What if we can be joy in everything we do?
- What can be created from the space of kindness?
- What if I didn't take myself so seriously?
- How much can we change?

The Energy of Creativity

- What would you enjoy changing?
- Could you be the smile someone has not yet had today?

Are we receiving the molecules joyfully through our bodies, being and ideas of possibility? Where else can we go and what else can be born from this? What if every creation was a dance with the molecules of possibility?

The more I do, the more I desire to do. I was made wrong for having 15 different projects going on. "Sit down and rest. You have too much going on. You're always doing something. Why don't you relax?" For me, the more I've got going on, the more energized I am and the more ideas come flooding in. And the invitations continue to come in for collaborations.

What else can be born with this idea that's brewing? Where else can I go? Creation creates more. When you are in the creation zone, ideas are zinging all over the place. What choices can be made from these creations? Is now the time for the creation or is it later?

Are you willing to be inconceivable and undefinable? Are you willing to be joy? Are you willing to jump in without knowing how to do it? If it feels joyous, would you like to follow that joy? If nothing is inconceivable, then what could be generated?

If you were choosing your life from the inconceivable and undefinable, what would you create? Are you ready for infinite possibilities beyond anything you can imagine?

I ask the Universe to contribute to my life. To bring the people who desire contribution, collaboration, co-creation, fun and more! Do I know how this will show up or who will be calling or emailing me? Not a clue!

Follow the energy of the ideas. They could be breadcrumbs sprinkled down a path you never noticed before. Do yourself and your opportunities a favor and stay out of conclusion and judgments. When you conclude, the flow of ideas and creativity halts to a slow trickle (if any). One idea can build onto another idea, and so on. It can lead you to other people to include in the creation or to ask questions for more inspiration.

You never know when you will inspire creations for other people. I was in my first Facilitator training sharing some personal insights and questions. That vulnerability sparked the idea in a new friend for collaboration with me. Literally, within a week, we created a radio show together where none had existed before.

Another time a friend and I were running a yummy body process and someone walked by and I cracked a joke. That joke opened up some sticking points that we processed each other on for a good hour. This encounter led to creating a 6 part telecall series. How amazing! We followed the energy with no point of view for the outcome.

I have made a lot of choices in my life where I had absolutely no idea what I was doing and jumped off the cliff of the unknown. Push the crap and all the reasons why you shouldn't jump off to the side. I'm jumping off the deep end – here I gooooooooo! Jump and land in the beautiful water and know that the Universe has your back. OK, now what? I'm in the water; my body goes down a bit in the water and then comes up to the surface. I don't think about it – I am being. I'm swimming, paddling, maybe looking for the waves to surf. Imagine this space of total expansiveness of riding the wave with no conclusion of

The Energy of Creativity

where the waves will take you. Ahhhhhhh.

And what if it doesn't show up as elegantly and joyfully as this description? What if you jump and your foot gets stuck in the mud? OK, now what do I do? How do I dislodge my foot from the mud? I'm out of the mud now. I have mud all over my clothes? Now what? What can we create from being completely covered in the mud? Mud art! Mud pies! Embrace being covered in mud, giggle at the mud. If you can stay out of the conclusion of this is what always happens to me so I'm not going to do anything, what can unfold in front of you?

The adventure of living and creation – I have no idea what this is going to look like. Being willing to make more choices than ever before – what else can I choose? What else can I create?

If all my creations showed up the way I thought they would, how small would the creations be? Thinking about it from that angle is quite funny to me. Is there any reason I would limit what they could become?

Allow energy to flow all around your creations. What if you drop all your barriers and allow yourself to be totally vulnerable? Would you consider dancing with the molecules of possibility? Put your mind on a holiday and allow whatever desires to be born to happen. When you restrict yourself and decide before you even start that your idea is stupid, has no merit or whatever you decide, you've locked away any possibility for something greater to happen.

What if your first idea spawns a whole bunch of other ideas? What if what you create is a contribution for someone else? What if you share that idea with the people that pop into your awareness? What can be created from that?

What joyous, generative juicy creations are waiting for you to hear their whispers? The whispers of possibility await you.

How much fun can you have playing and dancing with the molecules that so generously desire to contribute to you? The quantum entanglements desire to rearrange themselves in total contribution to your desires. Wikipedia defines quantum entanglement as a physical phenomenon that occurs when pairs or groups of particles are generated or interact in ways such that the quantum state of each particle cannot be described independently—instead, a quantum state may be given for the system as a whole.

You create YOU! You create your life. What if there is no definition of you? What if it's an adventure to create you?

Ideas that come into our awareness are creations. We choose to act on some of these ideas. I get so many ideas all the time that I write them down on my phone or in a journal so the ideas are there to commune with.

Some questions to leave you with:

- What gifts do you have waiting to be opened as if by magic?
- What creative capacities have I ignored?
- What if you allowed the Universe to flow through you and contribute to everything? What if that is the greatest magic and contribution to you, your life and living?

Greater comes to those who ask for it. Are you asking for greater? What energy, space and consciousness can you and your body be to live a joyful, creative life? Whatever that means in your world. Are you ready to create more adventures? Are you ready to create the adventure of you? Have a blast!

About the Author

BETSY MCLOUGHLIN

Betsy McLoughlin is a best-selling author, a dynamic facilitator and Coach. She believes in the play and magic of possibilities, using both to completely transform her life by releasing depression and many other illnesses. She has created a life of joy, lightness, fun, and expansion. Betsy facilitates and empowers others to create the same in her coaching practice and in the many classes she teaches as an Access Consciousness® Certified Facilitator, Access Body Process and Bars Facilitator, Right Body For You® Taster Facilitator, and change agent of magnitude. She believes in the possibilities of generating the life you desire; she has witnessed amazing transformations and is honored to be part of their team.

Betsy is also a magical Realtor who enjoys playing differently in real estate. Her calm demeanor, willingness to ask questions and look for what else is possible creates opportunities for her clients that might not be there without her involvement. Betsy is a co-host of the Radio

The Energy of Creativity

Show "Imperfect Brilliance" on A2Zen.fm where she and her co-hosts Sadie Lake and Kathy Williams explore embracing your supposed imperfections to create beyond what you thought was possible.

Betsy lives in Damascus, MD with her husband and crazy fun dog Zeke. She loves spending time with her son Matthew, traveling, meeting new people, gardening and enjoying life.

You can reach Betsy at accessbetsy@gmail.com or find her on Facebook and on her Imperfect Brilliance Page. Betsy coaches in person as well as facilitates remote sessions from anywhere in the world. Betsy would love to travel to your area and hold some classes for you. You can find her at www.betsymcloughlin.accessconsciousness.com. Her website is www.creatingyumminess.com, www.imperfectbrilliance.com.

Chapter 13

BORN TO BE CREATIVE

By Erica Glessing

I hated Barbie dolls. I would play with trolls, dressing them up in outfits carved out of flower petals. I would braid the troll hair and I loved all the different colors. My mom would take us to the beach on the weekends and summers, and we would play for hours building sand castles and creating art out of driftwood and seaweed.

Every creative move I made as a child was celebrated until I became an adult – out of control, impossible to follow, creative at every corner. I have a memory of a college English teacher giving me a grade on a paper about getting into basketball pickup games. We had to write a how-to paper, I guess I was the only girl who chose pickup basketball. I remember her saying "I'm not sure how to grade this but I would like to reward your creativity."

So it's not surprising that I became the spark of energy that I am today. A few places along the way my creativity got me into trouble. I remember in high school, I amended my own physical education curriculum to get credit for riding my horse instead of going to PE class. I created a curriculum for biology too, but instead of doing the creative curriculum for biology, I just pretty much didn't go to class. I built my own English curriculum around books that I liked and desired to read. I would just keep making suggestions until the teachers gave me a lot of space to create and generate outside of any box that would try to keep me.

My first career as a news reporter again celebrated creativity, to a point. I would come up with stories first, original, and I didn't read other journalist's stories for my research. I would always go to the source and find everything out new and fresh. I had psychic ability and would always be someplace where news would happen. This wasn't always enjoyable, I remember getting to the scene of a crime where a gun club owner had fired a shot at boys "doing donuts" in the dirt on his property. One of the boys ended up with a bullet in his neck, and I got there before the police or ambulance. In the long run the boy survived, and the gun club owner was slapped on the wrist – being there first, I sat with the boy and comforted him. I always had a sense for news that took me to the place where news would happen.

Mixing Creative with Psychic

Creativity and psychic ability are an interesting mix, because you know things you know that no one else seems to know – and then you take that information and play with it and interact with it in ways that no one else does – until you don't fit in anywhere easily. Your creativity can actually be something that makes it impossible for you to function as a "minion" on the planet, so if you are relating to anything I'm sharing, get that your creativity is exactly what the world is calling for on the planet today – even when things look different for you than anyone else.

The Energy of Creativity

The major life change that happened for me in early 2013 was reading a book called "Driven by Distraction" by Edward Hallowell. I read the book and recognized that the way my brain functions can be characterized as a "race car" brain. This awareness of what works for me – constant change, constantly adding new projects, constantly taking on more than the average person – has changed everything about my success in every area of my life! This was followed by landing up on the tools of Access Consciousness®, another game-changing experience where I found creative, psychic and even wilder people than I am, to play with on the planet.

I get that I am one of those people for whom being creative comes naturally. It's hard for me to even "get" what I do or how I can see things that no one else sees, or who is willing to make combinations that no one else considers. In jobs, this would serve me well and drive others crazy, at the same time. No one ever knew exactly where I was, or how I achieved any of my achievements.

I Was Fired from My Last Corporate Job

The last corporate position I held, I worked for a foundation dedicated to early cancer detection research. I was able to double the fundraising results (or be a part of a team that did) with creative marketing. I just couldn't show the linear path to achieve what I was able to create and generate. It was more like putting a puzzle together and I knew how to do it, including ranking the organization on the internet, for its keywords, for the first time in its history. I couldn't "teach" what I was doing because it meant being interactive, alive, and being so much fun that everyone joined in to the events that year in record numbers. I lost that position ultimately, not being able to prove how the fundraising went from $500,000 to

$1,000,000 with the marketing that I was able to build and generate.

Yet, as I look back, I am so joyful that I left, because that led me back to my own company, a book publishing house, where I can publish and support writers who are creating outside of their own boxes, and generating creativity in their own lives.

Before I lost that position, I was thinking that as a single mom, I had to be a certain way or act a certain way or carry a certain job or basically hate life to live life and survive. Once I lost that position, I went into a new definition and commitment to myself. I had an understanding that each and every person has gifts and possibly the more awake we become, the less easy we are to define.

Out of Control, Out of Definition

Now let's take this energy of being in the entrepreneurial space, and even in this space, there are lots of messages to become dedicated to one "niche" or one focus area and once you succeed in that space, you are encouraged to get bigger.

I would look at the people I admired, though, and they would be running six or seven companies. The people that I could relate to were succeeding with a lot going on and not any one specific niche that they could be pinned down into. The funny thing is that once I said "I talk to spirit," and let my psychic ability shine, and coupled that with my book publishing skills, the world opened up exponentially for me.

I stopped trying not to be this and to be that and when someone tries to pin it down again, I say, "I'm out of control and out of definition." It happened for me again recently, I started a group on connecting to spirit, and one of the people said "is this for connecting to spirit as a whole, or the spirits of people who have crossed over, or what?" I answered "what if we don't define that."

What if every time someone wants to pin you down you just laugh and ask them what it would be like to be out of definition? To be so expansive that any one name could never capture you?

The funny thing is that for you it could be generative to be in one area of definition, like, for instance, a wizard at ceramics, or a brilliant business coach. What if you allowed people to be in a "niche" or to be "too much fun to niche" or just allowed everyone to generate what works for them?

We had this conversation in a class I was teaching last week. I dreamed about it the night after I taught it – it was such a powerful dream too. The trigger was an ad I saw that said "You must have Instagram in Your Business." Or something like that, why every business is required to have "Instagram," a social media tool.

I let the class know that the moment you hear "you must do something one way" you can perceive a lie. There's never any one way to do anything, that's the anti-creativity.

Creativity in Social Media

One of the areas where I shine is in social media. My Facebook fan page has upwards of 58,000 fans, and I have followers on YouTube, Twitter and lots of wonderful Facebook friends. I'm sure they never have an exact idea of what's going to show up next on my walls and in my videos. One morning I shared messages from the spirit of Michael Jackson, another I share book publishing tips. How much fun can I have sharing messages that aren't expected? And mixing that up with messages that might be expected? Oh now that for me is great fun.

So here's a fun way you can determine how to build your social media following strategy. Make a pie, and give it percentages relating to all of the social media tools you might want to embrace in your world. So, for me, it's Facebook, YouTube, and Twitter. I'm not getting much joy from Instagram, and Pinterest and LinkedIn don't rock my world. The direction I'm getting from spirit is to play with Facebook and Twitter big time in the year to come, with some YouTube joy thrown in for fun. I'm also being shown to embrace radio, but I haven't integrated that message into my life yet except to appear as a guest on radio shows that invite me in.

For a few years, my strategy around Twitter was not to tweet. That was a good strategy because I didn't get the platform. Now I'm seeing it as a really fun place to shine, so I'm letting myself have more time in that medium than in the past.

I'm suggesting that you look at your own business, or your own direction, and see when and if social media can work to grow it – and not to accept the "rote" suggestions that you find written everywhere. As you choose based originally on your own gut feeling, your own perceptions, and your own knowledge of the strengths and weaknesses of your own gifts – you can use social media much more effectively. I remember one real estate person I coached on this was trying to write blogs, even though he hated writing, and was not a native English speaker. His native country didn't use written language too much, so, speaking for him was natural and writing was a steep climb. We brainstormed a video (VLOG) approach and he started creating video "ah ha" moments and this took his whole world to the next level. It was so different than hiring someone to write blogs about real estate that weren't his own "ah ha" moments. Because what people love about him is his insight into life and living – with real estate woven into the whole, in a graceful and beautiful way.

Nurturing Awareness as a Tool for Creativity

So back to my dream, I dreamed the whole concept of being in conclusion, and saw how that blocks awareness. Every time you conclude something like "I'm not creative," it blocks your creativity. Every time you buy into a philosophy of anything being a solid wall of definition around your choices, you block awareness. So if you read the ad "Every business needs Instagram," and in your psyche, you buy into that concept, that it must be true, you could spend eons trying to figure out how to make an image tool (Instagram is image-based) fit your demographic audience that still likes words too. For me, I like mixing it up, and I just basically don't listen to any of the experts. I might read or listen to the experts but not to take what they are doing and "rinse and repeat" the steps, but to take what they are doing, and then listen to my world, my businesses, my offerings, my own Erica-ness, my own awareness, and then build something out of me that is not anything I've actually seen created in the same mix, in a new way.

This awareness of what works for me is funny, because then I become an expert even on this. So I was coaching someone the other day, and I said that she could benefit from having four or five orgasms every day. Then I said "unless your body doesn't want that then you should listen to your body and honor what is asking for, even if it is going against my advice of experiencing life more fully waist down." My intuition had show me she was living from the solar plexus up – and was not accepting awareness from the belly button down. Not that I am any kind of expert on orgasms, I just was able to perceive what could be stopping her success because I was willing to have an awareness that would serve her – even in a topic area taboo for most business consultations.

Whatever isn't working for you, trust it's not fun. Whatever is working for you, is more likely more fun. This doesn't mean you can't be on a learning curve, because a learning curve isn't fun sometimes. Yet, when you are creating with awareness, it's different.

You might wake up asking questions, like "what would my body like today? How can I out create yesterday? What would my business like today? What could I create today that I didn't create yesterday?"

Then when you ask, just go about your day, and when some path seems brighter than the other path, take one you haven't taken, and see what that feels like. Or take a path you have taken, but order something different from the menu.

Mix it Up

And if nothing has worked yet, mix up 27 things every day. Move six or seven things around your house differently, wash dishes differently, drive to work differently, do your hair differently. If you choose 27 things differently every day for 27 days, your life will not be the same. I challenge you!

About the Author

Erica Glessing

Erica Glessing is so far outside of the box that the box had to change and she no longer fits any definitions. The bio changes so fast she can't keep up with it. None of her websites are updated because she keeps having major successes. In 2015, 85 authors who were published by Happy Publishing, where she is the CEO, became #1 bestselling authors. She is the mom to three beautiful children, all of whom think outside the box. You can find her on Twitter @ericaglessing; friend her on Facebook @ericaglessing, and check out her offerings at www.HappyPublishing.net, but don't expect them to be all that she does or all that she offers. Her spirit work can be seen on YouTube @ericaglessing.

www.ingramcontent.com/pod-product-compliance
Lightning Source LLC
Chambersburg PA
CBHW032300150426
43195CB00008BA/521